The Middle Fork of the S...
A Compreh

Warning

The Middle Fork of the Salmon is a wild, free-flowing river that can flood every spring when melting snow swells the channel. Rapids may change and evolve over time. This guidebook is NOT meant to be the final word on running the rapids of the Middle Fork. Rapid diagrams and descriptions provide suggestions on how to run the whitewater. They are not exact. Scout rapids and make final decisions for yourself. This guidebook cannot compensate for poor judgement and inadequate preparation.

The landscape surrounding the Middle Fork is a Wilderness and is subject to a wide variety of natural hazards. The hiking routes and other activities covered in these pages are meant to provide general suggestions for your enjoyment while floating the Middle Fork. Take into consideration all factors including weather conditions and personal skills when trying any activity suggested in

©2006 Matt Leidecker
First Printing - 2006

Idaho River Publications LLC
105 Triumph Circle Hailey, ID 83333

Printed by Colorwest in Burbank, California

Additional copies can be ordered at - www.mattlphoto.com
Please send questions and comments to - mfguidebook@mattlphoto.com

Middle Fork geology map courtesy of the United States Geologic Society
http://pubs.usgs.gov/imap/i-2765/i-2765_1.pdf

All maps created with TOPO! software ©2006 National Geographic.
To learn more visit: http://www.nationalgeographic.com/pp

All photographs and artwork by Matt Leidecker

Front cover: Weber Rapid in August
Back Cover (top down): Looking down on Sheepeater Camp; A lone kayaker enjoys the view below Ship Island; Stoking the fire at Otter Bar; Drifting below Ramshorn rapid; A paddle boat takes a hit in Rubber

ISBN # 1-4243-0266-8

Introduction

In 1991 I was fortunate to join the crew of a commercial outfitter on the Middle Fork of the Salmon. The perfect summertime college job turned into a career of 15 consecutive guiding seasons. Over that time I had the opportunity to work with many great Middle Fork boatmen (and women). My early career as a guide was given a jump start by learning from their years of river experience.

My connection with the river broadened while studying geology at Middlebury College. When a thesis project threatened to steal several weeks from my guiding season, I proposed to study the effects of glaciers on the Middle Fork canyon. My thesis advisor, an avid fisherman, thought it was a great idea. During the summer of 1996 I snuck away from camp obligations to gather data at hundreds of sites along the river. A weeklong research trip helped complete the initial study.

Our discoveries (discussed later in the guide) opened my eyes to a different way of seeing the canyon landscape. Since completing our work, several rain-induced landslides have altered the river channel. Watching the evolution of these events has been one of the highlights of my guiding career. This recent geologic activity, combined with a desire to share my research, has been one of the motivating factors behind writing this book.

In 1996 I started taking photographs on the river, which provided an additional perspective of the Middle Fork Canyons. While creating images to share with family and friends I fell in love with photography. As my slide collection grew I started to envision a book of Middle Fork photographs. After several years that dream was realized with the publication of "Impassable Canyon – Journey Down the Middle Fork of the Salmon" in December 2002.

My connection with the river deepened as it continued to wrap me in its sinewy embrace. On every trip I set out to discover something new. I hiked to take pictures, and every ridge I climbed opened my eyes to new possibilities across the river. The view from up high provided a unique perspective to see the geology and dynamics of a natural, free-flowing river system. My job as a guide was to share this beautiful place with others. Organizing my knowledge into a comprehensive guidebook would share my experiences with a wider audience.

This guidebook is divided into four sections: Orientation, River Maps, Hiking, and Geology. The Orientation provides the reader with information essential to planning a Middle Fork Trip. The River Maps are the meat and potatoes of the guide. These beautiful maps (accompanied by a full page of text) provide a wealth of visual information. The Hiking Section describes over 130 routes that are drawn on the river maps. The Geology Section includes a history of the rocks along the Middle Fork and descriptions of the geologic points-of-interest marked on the maps.

For many people the opportunity to float the Middle Fork is an once-in-a-lifetime experience. This comprehensive book offers something for every level of Middle Fork user. Novice and expert rafters will find detailed descriptions for running the significant rapids at high and low water. Hikers may be inspired to try an adventurous climb. History buffs will discover convenient points of interest listed along the maps, and photographers may appreciate my suggestions of scenic viewpoints. The geology information is gleaned from original research, discovery, and first hand observations. It is presented here for the first time to a wider, river savvy audience.

Please keep in mind that this guide is written from a unique perspective of familiarity and comfort within the Middle Fork Canyon. The rapid descriptions are not the final word and runs may change over time. With a strong climbing background and insatiable thirst for adventure, my comfort level on the longer and more exposed hikes may be a bit warped. Assess your personal fitness and comfort level when considering longer hikes or those that encounter steep terrain. It is better to turn around than risk an accident in the remote confines of the canyon. Remember, coming down is always harder than going up. As with any guidebook, there are bound to be errors in these pages. I would greatly appreciate any feedback, positive or negative, to improve on future editions.

Producing this book has been a very rewarding experience for me. As I start to phase out of a full time Middle Fork career it has been great to revisit 15 years of guiding memories. In the words of Clarence Stilwill, a veteran Middle Fork guide:

"You can leave a river you love, but it never leaves you."

Whether you are a grizzled veteran or first-year boater, I sincerely hope this book will enrich your Middle Fork experience.

Matt Leidecker
April 2006

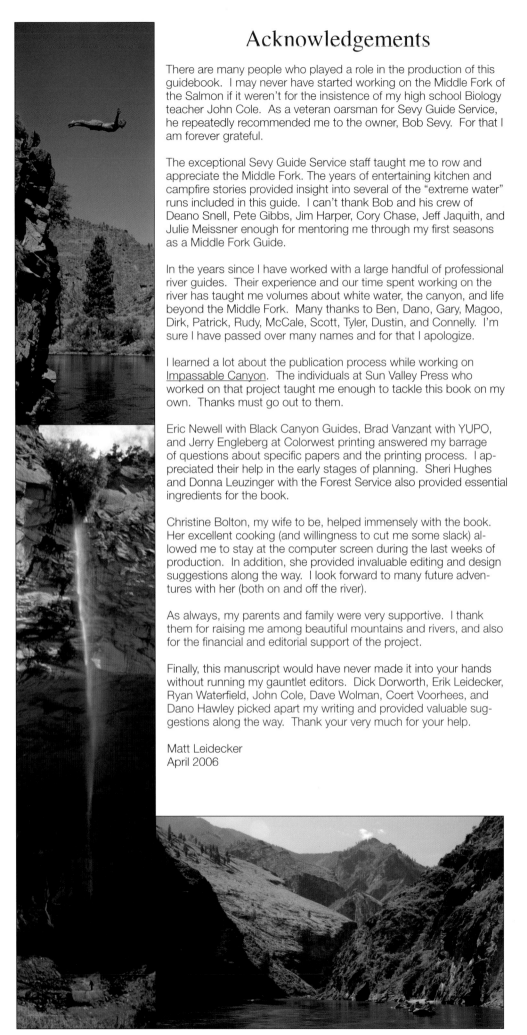

Acknowledgements

There are many people who played a role in the production of this guidebook. I may never have started working on the Middle Fork of the Salmon if it weren't for the insistence of my high school Biology teacher John Cole. As a veteran oarsman for Sevy Guide Service, he repeatedly recommended me to the owner, Bob Sevy. For that I am forever grateful.

The exceptional Sevy Guide Service staff taught me to row and appreciate the Middle Fork. The years of entertaining kitchen and campfire stories provided insight into several of the "extreme water" runs included in this guide. I can't thank Bob and his crew of Deano Snell, Pete Gibbs, Jim Harper, Cory Chase, Jeff Jaquith, and Julie Meissner enough for mentoring me through my first seasons as a Middle Fork Guide.

In the years since I have worked with a large handful of professional river guides. Their experience and our time spent working on the river has taught me volumes about white water, the canyon, and life beyond the Middle Fork. Many thanks to Ben, Dano, Gary, Magoo, Dirk, Patrick, Rudy, McCale, Scott, Tyler, Dustin, and Connelly. I'm sure I have passed over many names and for that I apologize.

I learned a lot about the publication process while working on Impassable Canyon. The individuals at Sun Valley Press who worked on that project taught me enough to tackle this book on my own. Thanks must go out to them.

Eric Newell with Black Canyon Guides, Brad Vanzant with YUPO, and Jerry Engleberg at Colorwest printing answered my barrage of questions about specific papers and the printing process. I appreciated their help in the early stages of planning. Sheri Hughes and Donna Leuzinger with the Forest Service also provided essential ingredients for the book.

Christine Bolton, my wife to be, helped immensely with the book. Her excellent cooking (and willingness to cut me some slack) allowed me to stay at the computer screen during the last weeks of production. In addition, she provided invaluable editing and design suggestions along the way. I look forward to many future adventures with her (both on and off the river).

As always, my parents and family were very supportive. I thank them for raising me among beautiful mountains and rivers, and also for the financial and editorial support of the project.

Finally, this manuscript would have never made it into your hands without running my gauntlet editors. Dick Dorworth, Erik Leidecker, Ryan Waterfield, John Cole, Dave Wolman, Coert Voorhees, and Dano Hawley picked apart my writing and provided valuable suggestions along the way. Thank your very much for your help.

Matt Leidecker
April 2006

Table of Contents

Introduction 4
Acknowledgments 5
Overview Map 7

Orientation
    Permit and Lottery Information 8
    Cancellations 8
    Fee Information 8
    Forest Service Regulations 8
    Tributary Information 8
    Stanley, ID 8
    River Access 9
    Car Shuttles 9
    About the Middle Fork 9
    Rapids and Classifications 10
    Other Safety Considerations 11
    Rapid Names 12
    Rapid Diagrams 12
    Fishing 12
    Hazards 13
    Water Temperature and Weather 13
    Emergencies 13
    Floating With Kids 14
    Camps and Reservation system 14
    Cultural Considerations 14
    GPS Coordinates 14
    Boundary Creek Launch Site Facilities 15
    Daggar Falls 15
    River Etiquette 16
    Cache Bar Take out 17
    Using This Guide 17
        Maps 17
        Kayaking 17
        Hiking 18
        Geology 18
        Photography 18
        History 20
    River Flows 20
    Selected Middle Fork Flows Graph 21
    Selected Middle Fork Snowpack Graph 21

River Maps
    River Map Introduction 22
    Mile by Mile Descriptions 24-65
    Rapid Diagrams 49
    Rapid Diagrams 59

Hiking Section
    Hiking Descriptions 66-77

Geology Section
    Geologic History of the Middle Fork 78-85
    Mile-by-Mile Geology Descriptions 85-93

Notes Page 94
Related Books 95

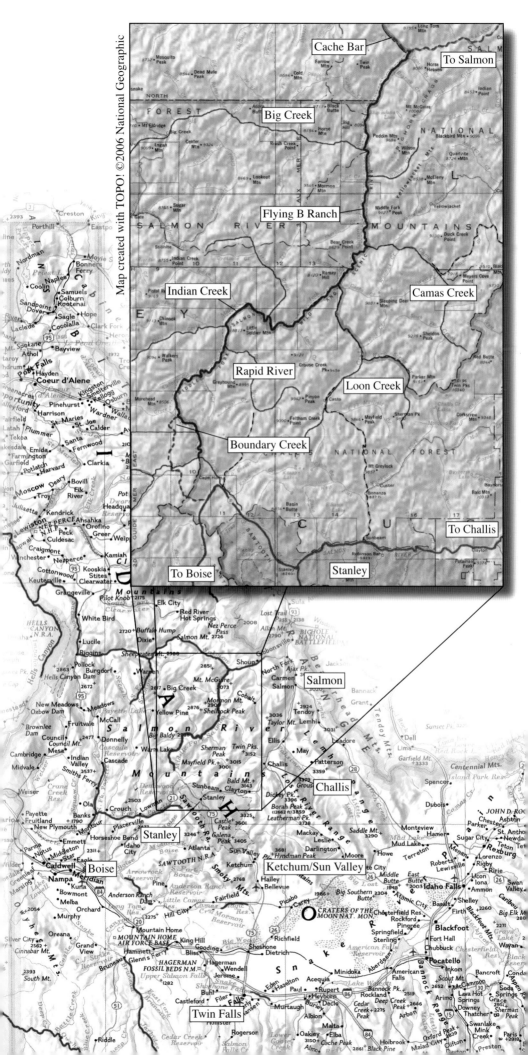

Permit and Lottery Info

A Middle Fork Ranger District (MFRD) permit is required to float the Middle Fork, a Wild and Scenic river that bi-sects the Frank Church River of No Return Wilderness. Permits for private boaters are allocated through a combination lottery/call-in basis. The lottery control season is May 28 through September 3rd. Applications are accepted between Dec 1 and Jan 31 and results are announced by mail in February. Pre and post-season permits are issued by telephone only on a first-come, first-serve basis beginning October 1st (or the first working day in October).

Cancellations

A permit holder who cannot make the trip must provide a written cancellation to the MFRD office 21 days prior to the launch date to avoid a no-show penalty. A no-show penalty restricts the right to have a permit on the Middle Fork for three years.

Cancelled permits are re-allocated by telephone only on a first-come, first-serve basis after the initial lottery results are announced in February.

Fee Info

There is a $6.00 non-refundable fee to enter the lottery that applies to call-in permits as well. The Forest Service charges a $4.00/person per day user fee for any portion of a day spent on the river. Payments must be made to the MFRD three days prior to the launch date. Any last minute additions may pay with a credit card at the Boundary Creek launch site.

Forest Service Regulations and Requirements

There is a lot of fine print that applies to every group and permit holder so review the Forest Service permit package materials thoroughly. Refer to the MFRD office or website for further questions. (see address below)

The MFRD does a great job of managing over 10,000 people who float through the Frank Church Wilderness every summer. Their job is very important and helps protect the pristine nature of this Wild and Scenic River.   The launch personnel are required to inspect all of the following pieces of equipment. Self support kayakers should review the recommendations regarding these requirements at the MFRD website.

- Toilet system and capacity appropriate for the group size.
- Fire pan and ash container.
- Food strainer fine enough to filter coffee grounds.
- Shovel, Axe, and Bucket to help extinguish any campfires.

MFRD personnel will give your group an orientation before leaving Boundary Creek. The talk reviews information already given to the permit holder and addresses low impact camping practices. Please follow their suggestions or requirements for handing garbage, human waste, and soap while using the corridor.

Middle Fork Ranger District Contact Info
Hwy. 93 N. (UPS and FedEx)
P.O. Box 750
Challis, ID 83226-0750
Info/Available Permits – 208.879.4101
Application Requests – 208.879.4112
Fax – 208-879-4198
Web – www.fs.fed.us/f4/sc

Tributary Info

There are several Middle Fork tributaries with navigable whitewater runs. They include: Marsh Creek, Rapid River, Loon Creek, Camas Creek, and Big Creek. Marsh is the most frequently run, as it provides the only access to the upper Middle Fork when the Boundary Creek road is snowed in. These creeks are always changing, often have debris and log jams, and should only be attempted by expert rafters with small, light boats. Permits for the Middle Fork are required once reaching the main stem of the river anywhere between Daggar Falls and the Confluence.

A Middle Fork permit is not required for parties running Big Creek if the party floats out to the confluence in one day with no overnight stays along the Middle Fork corridor. A Big Creek Tributary permit is required. Contact the Krassel Ranger District at 208.634.0600.

Stanley, ID

The last civilized stop before heading into the Boundary Creek launch site is Stanley, ID. From Boise or McCall it is possible to drive directly into Boundary Creek. To make arrangements with the shuttle service, however, it is best to plan a stop in this charming mountain town.

Stanley's year round population is less than 100, and the summer population closes in on several hundred. It is the whitewater capital of central Idaho and the operational base for several Main Salmon day-trip and Middle Fork commercial outfitters. The main gas station/grocery store/hotel is the Mountain Village complex on Highway 21. Quantities may vary, but a decent selection of fresh produce and last minute items are available. Don't plan on shopping for an entire trip out of Stanley. Jerry's Country Store, downriver 1 mile in Lower Stanley on Highway 93, has a smaller selection and some specialty items. Lodging in the Stanley valley is usually booked well in advance. Consider making reservations if you wish to spend a night in Stanley. There are several restaurants, and a great local bakery in "downtown" Stanley that should not be missed.

Contact the Stanley Chamber of Commerce Website at www.stanleycc.org or call 800.878.7950 for more information.

Sunlight illuminates Stanley between afternoon storms.

River Access

The Forest Service road into Boundary Creek is snowed in until late May/early June, depending on the year. (Call the Middle Fork Ranger District office for the road status) When the road is closed, the two options are to float Marsh Creek or use a backcountry flying service to access the launch ramp at Indian Creek.

Car Shuttles

Running your own Middle Fork shuttle adds a day to your trip. Consider enlisting the help of some non river-running friends to join you for the scenic drive into Boundary Creek, fishing or hiking along the river and the pre-trip campfire festivities. They will leave Cache Bar the following morning for the spectacular drive down the Salmon River which has recreational opportunities and hot spring soaks along the way. Catching a ride back to Stanley is relatively easy with multiple trips taking out at Cache Bar on a daily basis. Space is limited so please leave only one vehicle parked at Cache Bar. There is additional parking along the river road upstream.

If you can't convince a friend, the follow businesses offer river shuttle services. Some raft parties may use a local air charter service to access the Indian Creek Launch site at very high and very low water.

Shuttle Services

River Shuttles: 208.774.4188
North Fork Store: 208.865.2412
Sawtooth Transportation: 208.774.2323
Rawhide Outfitters: 208.756.4276
Blackadar Boating: 208.756.3958

Air Charter Services

McCall Aviation: 800.992.6559
Middle Fork Aviation: 208.879.5728
Salmon Air Taxi: 800.448.3413
Arnold Aviation: 208.382.4844

About the Middle Fork

The Middle Fork of the Salmon River is one of the premier multi-day white water float trips in the world. It cuts through a spectacular and rugged canyon wilderness with beautiful scenery and white water challenges from late April through early November. It has something for all river runners: early and late season trips offer isolation; May and June are packed with fast water thrills; July's moderate mid-season flows are popular with many rafters; and low water technical challenges follow in August and September. Kayakers find ample opportunities for play, hikers can follow gentle trails or challenge themselves on steep ridgelines, and photographers discover endless compositions as light plays across the canyon landscape (see more on photography below).

The gin clear waters of the Middle Fork contribute to it's beauty.

The Middle Fork flows 100 miles through three distinct ecological regions. Boundary Creek launch is in a high alpine forest just below 6000 feet. The first 25 miles are dominated by swift channels and numerous rapids. Thick forests of Lodgepole Pine and Douglas Fir trees line the banks. Below Indian Creek (mile 25) the river opens up and majestic Ponderosa Pine trees flank the river corridor. The hills are more gentle and open, the rapids calm and subdued. Below the Flying B Ranch (mile 67) the river plunges into a deep lower gorge. The walls narrow overhead and the river crashes through "Impassable Canyon," the third deepest in North America.

There are numerous whitewater challenges along this 100 mile stretch. As on any free-flowing river, they change with the water level. Below is a brief description of the river's navigation challenges at various flow levels.

** It is important to note that the character of the river will be quite different if it is rising or falling. The Middle Fork at 4 feet and rising is a more aggressive and unpredictable beast than at 4 feet on the downside of a peak.**

Extreme Water (Above 7 feet)

Every river is dangerous at or above its bank full stage. The Middle Fork starts to exhibit flood characteristics above 7 feet on the river gauge, gnawing into the banks and toppling whole trees into the current which is already full of wood and debris deposited by winter avalanches. Eddies are often washed out and those that remain have violent shear lines. The water strains through riverbank vegetation and low timbered benches like Hospital Bar and Survey Camp. Common rapids may be washed out while huge, unexpected waves catch boaters unaware. It is a challenge to maintain good position in the river as it sweeps around blind corners and into unexpected hazards.

I have noted some extreme white water hazards, but reading a guidebook is not adequate preparation for running the Middle Fork at flows above 7 feet. Seriously contemplate your group's preparation and ability to deal with dangerous conditions.

High Water (5 feet to 7 feet)

There is a significant difference between 5 feet and 7 feet, but the river is confined within its banks, no longer a chaotic flood full of woody debris. With the exception of the upper canyon (Boundary to Indian Creek) floating at this level is pretty straightforward. Many rapids are washed out, and there is generally plenty of room to avoid the big hydraulics. Exceptions remain, however, and high water should be approached with caution.

The upper canyon is swift, narrow, and choked with rapids. At high water the first twelve miles is a class IV+ river with class V consequences. Infrequent eddies and icy water make can turn a flip at Murphs Hole or Velvet Falls into a very serious situation. Most commercial outfitters avoid this section above 6 feet. Choosing to launch from

Taking a hit in rubber rapid at high water (6 feet).

Boundary Creek above this level requires preparation and a strong team.

The hazards at extreme and high flows are compounded by the icy water temperatures. An accident that dumps people in the river is extremely hazardous.

Moderate Water (3 feet to 5 feet)

Comtemplating the low water route through Haystack in 2003.

This is a great introductory level for Middle Fork boaters. The rapids still pack a punch, but slower water and warmer temperatures allow more time to recover from mistakes. Larger rocks come out so the wrap hazard does increase at moderate flows. Around 3 feet many rapids are more technical but lack the problematic rock gardens of low water.

Low Water (below 3 feet)

Below 3 feet the rapids on the Middle Fork enter their most technical stage. There are numerous rock gardens and some wrap hazards, but the water is moving slowly enough to allow for more response time. Below 2 feet there are several gravel shallows that defeat even the most skilled rafter. Some rapids become technically impossible to run without significant rubber wrestling.

Many groups fly into Indian Creek to start their low water Middle Fork trip. At levels below 2.5 feet the Upper Canyon is very technical and can be hard on both equipment and people. Those who launch from Boundary Creek should keep their boats light and plan extra time to navigate the numerous boulder gardens.

Rapids and Classifications

The rapids on the Middle Fork have been rated using the Standard European Classification system (see below). The difficulty of rapids may change drastically at different flows. I have described the high _and_ low water runs where appropriate. Rapids may change over time due to shifting gravel bars, ice movement in winter (upper canyon), or landslides that introduce boulders and other debris into the river channel. While thorough, this guide is not the final word.

I occasionally recommend a rowing technique of either a forward-push or back-pull for a particular run. Boaters attempting to row the Middle Fork at any water level should be well versed in both techniques. Safety recommendations included in the rapid descriptions sometimes note a good "rescue eddy" and identify problem areas for Inflatable Kayaks or IK's.

Standard European Rapid Classifications

- Class I: Very Easy – small regular waves and riffles; few or no obstacles; little maneuvering required.

- Class II: Easy – small waves with some eddies, low ledges, and slow rock gardens; some maneuvering required.

- Class III: Medium – numerous waves that are high and irregular; strong eddies; narrow, but clear passages that require expertise in maneuvering; scouting from the shore is necessary.

- Class IV: Difficult - long rapids with powerful, irregular waves, dangerous rocks, and boiling eddies; precise maneuvering and scouting from the shore imperative; take all possible safety precautions.

- Class V: Very Difficult – long rapids with wild turbulence and extremely congested routes that require complex maneuvering; a danger to your life and boat and near the limits of navigation.

- Class VI: The Limits of Navigation – rarely run; a definite hazard to your life.

Low Water Classifications

Rapids are marked with ticks that correspond to their class. Red ticks identify low water rapids that do not gain noteworthy status until the water drops below 3 feet. In addition to the European Classifications, I add these special "low water" classifications.

Empty boats clog the Chutes Rapid on a "deadhead" trip to Indian Creek.

- Low Water Shallows – Below 2 feet, finding the deep water channel in wide, flat stretches of river is not intuitive. Several "shallows" are noted throughout this guide with descriptions of where to find the deepest water. Getting stuck often requires dragging the boat into the deep channel.

- Low Water Class III – These rapids don't have large waves or strong eddies, but require precise rowing and quick moves through narrow, ill-defined channels. Lots of spinning, bouncing, and creative rowing techniques might be required.

Over the years I have found that running very soft tubes at low water helps immensely.

Other Safety Considerations

Whitewater rafting is a potentially dangerous activity and your group should take the necessary precautions to ensure a safe and enjoyable trip. Boating accidents can go from bad to worse in an instant, especially if your group is not prepared. It is important to discuss the contents of first aid, rescue, and wrap kits, as well as the rescue experience (or lack of) in the group. Assigning a rescue leader to handle emergency scenarios will minimize confusion in the chaos of a boating accident.

Each morning discuss the boating plan, major rapids, and the skill level of the group. Keep the boat behind you in sight at all times. This allows visual communication and prevents a lone raft from getting left behind in an emergency. Be on the lookout for downed trees and other log strainers along the banks. While on water safety is important, remember that the majority of injuries occur on shore while getting on and off the boats.

Getting stuck in rapids at low water on the Middle Fork is a common occurrence and nearly impossible to avoid at some levels. While not immediately dangerous, this situation can get very ugly if other boats in your party are following too closely. This may lead to rafts stacking on top of one another and can turn into a very hazardous situation. The phrase "use proper spacing" will accompany the description for rapids where this is a concern.

Rapid Names

The names of Middle Fork rapids change over time as individuals have made their mark on the canyon. Commercial groups often use different names depending on their lineage and pass them down through boatmen (or boatwomen). The Helfrich family of Oregon has the longest history on the river. Dave Helfrich and Cort Conley's historical guide provided several of the additional names included in this guide.

For continuity, rapid names were carried over from the Forest Service guide. Additional frequently used names are included in parentheses. Previously un-named rapids are identified by nearby features in the landscape, but a few rapids were given new names by the author's knowledge of common usage.

Rapid Diagrams

Detailed rapid diagrams are included for eight particularly challenging rapids encountered on the Middle Fork. These diagrams show the location of significant rocks and the predominate currents encountered AT LOW WATER. The flow regimes are similar at high water so one needs simply to imagine deeper water and faster current to extrapolate for high flows.

A Sample Diagram.

Fishing

The Middle Fork is renown for its native Cutthroat trout population. The Forest Service established strict catch-and-release regulations to protect the fishery as float boating gained popularity in the 70's and 80's. Anglers must present a current Idaho Fishing license at the request of Idaho Fish and Game Officers who patrol the river. Only single, barb-less hooks and artificial bait are permitted.

Fishing from a raft presents challenges to the oarsman, the angler, and the fish. Please follow these suggested guidelines to lessen the impact on the fishery.

For the Fish:
• Release the fish without removing it from the water. The use of a hands-free hook remover is the best way to accomplish this.
• If you must handle the fish, wet your hands first. This preserves the mucous like coating that protects the trout from disease.
• Pull your line from the river above rapids to prevent dragging the fish through whitewater.
• When releasing the fish, do it in the river, not over the raft to prevent dropping a fish into the bilge
• Keep a pair pliers or hemostat handy for releasing deeply set hooks.
• Check your barb-less hook by poking it through your shirt or short leg. If it snags upon revomal flatten it again.

For the Angler (and oarswoman!):
• Cast downstream. By the time you throw your line back upstream to a missed hole, your fly will look like a water skier to the laughing fish (this is not good)!
• Cast diagonally across the front of the boat to keep your captain's head free of hooks.
• On the off side, cast upstream and throw your line forward (downstream) on the back-cast. This will take some practice, but will open fishing opportunities on the other side of the raft.
• Keep your casts short and practice good line management as there is plenty for the fly line to get tangled on. Remember "less is more."
• Practice your "mending." The dual forces of moving water and raft will wreak havoc with fly line. Good mending will improve your presentation to the fish.
• When fishing from the boat all passengers should wear eye protection. Polarized lenses are best for the angler.

Fishing can be spotty in June and early July when the river is clouded by runoff. In late July and August, high temperatures tend to slow activity during the mid-day hours. The best Middle Fork fishing is in late August and Early September when the crystal clear water cools at the end of summer.

Fishing licenses are available at several locations in Stanley and you can also stock up on the classic Middle Fork fly patterns: Stimulator (stone fly imitation), Elk Hair Caddis, Adams Hopper (or other), Yellow and Red Humpy, and the Royal Wulff.

The remote the Impassable Canyon.

Hazards

Hypothermia.

Trips from late April to late June are subject to inclement weather and colder temperatures. The forty-degree water presents a legitimate risk of hypothermia, and even well dressed boaters have drowned after flips followed by long, exposed swims. Wear clothing appropriate for the conditions (wet or dry suits) and be prepared for swift water rescues.

Remote Environment

The Middle Fork, especially during the less crowded shoulder seasons (late April to mid May and mid September to early November) is an extremely remote environment. Emergency evacuation, even with a satellite phone, will take at least 6 hours to a full day, or more. Consider this reality when planning a trip and making decisions in the river corridor. CELL PHONES DO NOT WORK IN THE CANYON.

Sun-burn, Sun-rash and Dehydration

On commercial trips the most common cause of injury is the sun. To avoid bad sunburns, use sunscreen and re-apply halfway through the day if getting wet. SPF 15 is adequate for blocking the harmful rays.

Sunrash is a common problem after too much exposure to the sun, and may be aggrivated by 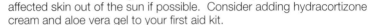 sunscreen with an SPF greater than 15. Cover up, stay cool and keep the affected skin out of the sun if possible. Consider adding hydracortizone cream and aloe vera gel to your first aid kit.

Don't tread on me!

Hydrate. Drink at least 2 quarts of water per day. Because they are floating all day rafters often forget to drink enough liquid and become dehydrated. This can often result in a headache or a nauseous feeling in camp. The solution is simple: re-hydrate.

Snakes, Bees, and other Wild Things

Wild animals such as black bear and rattlesnakes live in this wilderness. Remember, we are visitors here. It is unkind to harass the wildlife unless absolutely necessary for your own safety.

Pay attention to the yellowjackets in camp as they tend to congregate around the kitchen. Double check your soda can, beer or cocktail mug before the next sip. You may get a nasty sting on the lips or inside your mouth. The bees enjoy drinking gin and tonics, as do river guides.

The results of an intense microburst wind event.

Falling Trees

Mountainous terrain, intense local winds called "micro-bursts" and the shallow root systems of the massive Ponderosa Pine trees create a falling-tree hazard along the Middle Fork. Blown down trees have resulted in one death, a few close calls, and several damaged boats in my fifteen years on the Middle Fork. When the wind howls through a camp of Ponderosa Pines, the last place I want to be is in my tent. Stay alert, look around, and get ready to run in the right direction.

Water Temperature and Weather

These vary from season to season but as a rule of thumb:

April – Mid June: This is the rainy season. A spring boating party should be prepared to deal with the possibility of cold rain, snow, and icy water conditions. Storms may linger for a week or longer during the spring season.

Mid June – Mid July: The weather is usually warm and dry, though exceptions occur, and water temperature is bearable for short swims.

Mid July – September: It is generally hot and dry with a common buildup of afternoon thundershowers. Plan for the sudden weather changes associated with these storms including short, intense rain, hail and "micro-burst" wind storms. On sunny days, I often jump into the river to escape the heat and can stay for twenty minutes before getting chilled.

Emergencies

As mentioned, the Middle Fork is a remote

A stunning view of the river from the overlook above Rattlesnake Cave.

place and any rescue will not be quick, especially from a high ridgeline or scraggly canyon bottom. Consider carrying a satellite phone. The following locations have emergency radio contact with the outside world.

- Boundary Creek Guard Station
- Indian Creek Guard Station
- Middle Fork Lodge
- Thomas Creek Guard Station
- Loon Creek Ranch
- Flying B Ranch

During high season (June – August) there are at least six other groups launching on your same schedule. Another group will eventually float by and may be able to provide assistance. Be ready to flag them down. Most commercial outfitters carry satellite phones for emergencies.

Floating with Kids
Many companies have an arbitrary cut off age of 6 years old. Some six-year-olds behave like ten-year-olds and vice-versa, so this is a hard call. If a child is comfortable in water and has an adventurous spirit (most do) then six is fine. There are often more problems managing adults than children on commercial trips.

Because of the whitewater hazard, limit a kid heavy trip to lower water levels and float with competent rafters to reduce the chance of a flip or wrap. People float rivers like the Main Salmon with toddlers as young as 2 or 3, but I don't recommend the Middle Fork for such young children.

Camps and Camp Reservation System
Camping along the Middle Fork is controlled by a strict reservation system. Camps can be requested with the launch personnel at Boundary Creek starting at 3:30 PM the evening before your launch. If Boundary Creek is closed when you launch, your group must stop at Indian Creek (mile 25.5) to reserve camps with the ranger there.

A coin toss will determine the outcome between two groups who request the same camp. A group can challenge or be challenged only once for a camp. Flipping coins for camps can create animosity among parties. Share. There are no bad camps on the Middle Fork. Layover camps are approved on a case-by-case basis, depending on group size, season, and the camp chosen. Only one hot spring camp is allowed per group. Camp assignments will be finalized the morning before launch and written on the float permit. Only one camp per group is allowed below Big Creek.

Cultural Considerations
American Indians who called the Middle Fork canyon home were a branch of the Shoshone known as Tukuduka (two-kudu-kaa), or Sheepeaters. They lived comfortably in this rugged canyon for over 10,000 years, subsisting on a diet of wild meat and native plants. The encroachment of whites in the mid 1800's, and the military conflicts that ensued eventually forced the Tukuduka from their homeland.

There are hundreds of Tukuduka cultural sites along the Middle Fork of the Salmon River. Many are barely recognizable to the untrained eye. Nearly every flat bench by the river was utilized as a camp at one time, and red paintings or "pictographs" pepper rock overhangs throughout the canyon.

These sites are culturally significant to the present day ancestors of the Tukuduka so this guide notes only the commonly visited locations. Please explore them with respect and leave any artifacts you may find. Do not to touch any of the rock art, as the oils in fingers and hands can break down the pigment.

The following camps are located on historical Sheepeater encampments. The Boundary Creek staff will alert your group to any additional camping regulations at these sites.

- Lower Jackass Camp
- Pungo Camp
- White Creek Camp
- Rock island Camp
- Cow Camp

GPS Coordinates
All camps are labeled with easting and northing GPS coordinates in the UTM Zone 11 coordinate system. I took the waypoints off of the National Geographic TOPO! CD Rom and have included them for safety and rescue purposes. GPS users are bound to find minor discrepancies between them and coordinates they take in the canyon.

Gear piles up quickly at the Boundary Creek ramp.

Boundary Creek Launch Site Facilities
Campground
On the final descent to the river, you will pass a left turn into the campground. A one-way loop road accesses 13 campsites with water and restroom facilities. There is a $5.00 fee per night. Some sites have parking spaces deep enough to accommodate long trailers. Please choose another camp if you do not need a trailer space. The sites are closely spaced, so please respect other campers and keep any pre-trip celebration quiet after 10 PM. Of course, it always helps to invite the neighbors to join the festivities. Who knows, you may meet new boating friends.

Launch Unloading Area
The road in front of the launch ramp is a loop. Please keep it clear enough to allow vehicles with trailers to drive through, <u>at all times</u>. This means quickly unloading gear into your rig space and moving your car to the temporary parking area above. If you have a car battery operated blower, park to one side of the road, inflate the boats then move the car out of the way. Use your whole party to gang rig the heavy boxes and coolers onto your boats.

As a general rule, watch the commercial guides. They are experienced and usually have a clean and efficient system which has truck and trailer unloaded and out of the way in 20 minutes, allowing ample space to inflate boats and pre-rig frames and oars. There are those who are often unaware. If a group is clogging the road or acting in an inappropriate manner, smile and politely ask them to move. Expect others to do the same with your group.

Launch Ramp
The ramp is the only way to get your boat to the river so it becomes a point of congestion. Here are a few "Rules of the ramp:

- PRE-RIG as much of the boat (frames, floor boards, tables, oars) as possible before moving it onto the ramp.
- ORGANIZE the rest of the boat gear (coolers, boxes, dry bags, water jugs etc.) in a pile ready to load. Keep members of your group organized to help carry gear and move boats.
- SAFETY LINES used to lower the boat down the ramp should be prepped and ready to go.
- DO NOT BLOCK THE RAMP – Place the coolers and boxes in their holes, throw other gear onto the floor of the raft (sorry cat boaters) and get the boat down to the water. Any further organization and tying down should be done in the eddy below
- SHARE. This is a concept we should remember from kindergarten. If multiple groups have rafts ready to launch, alternate using the ramp.
- 5 MINUTES IS THE LONGEST YOUR BOAT SHOULD BE ON THE RAMP.
- SWEEP BOATS will take a bit longer to launch. Allow the commercial guides to get their big rigs down as soon as possible. It will clear a lot of rigging space.
- COMMUNICATE, chat, say hello, introduce yourself, and offer a hand. This goes a long way in helping maintain good ramp relations.

The launch ramp is steep and potentially dangerous. Move slowly when lowering boats and communicate with your group. A wet or recently oiled ramp can be very slippery. Check conditions before lowering. Generally, four agile people can lower a raft without needing a safety line, but if there are any concerns err on the cautious side and set one up. It's a bummer to begin a trip by losing a boat before it even hits water. The ramp road closes at 10PM.

Entering the Middle Fork in style!

Parking
There is a temporary parking lot on the uphill end of the ramp loop where cars can be parked during the launch process. Overnight vehicles must be moved to the campground or the long-term trailhead parking further up the road. The ramp scene starts out slowly in the morning but will quickly get crowded as buses of commercial guests start arriving. Please keep the loop drive clear at all times.

Water, Garbage and Restroom Facilities
Drinking water and restrooms are available at both the campground and launch ramp. There are no garbage services at Boundary Creek. Send your garbage out with the shuttle vehicles or pack it down the river.

Daggar Falls
There are fee campgrounds, water, and restroom facilities at the Daggar Falls site. There is a platform overlooking the falls from which you may be able to watch salmon migrating upstream. The best time of year for viewing the fish is Late June to Mid July.

River Etiquette

The Forest Service provides a few suggestions to rafting parties regarding river etiquette. Over the past 15 years I have developed my own opinions which you can take or leave:

Commercial vs. Private Use
The percentage of permit allocations are distributed roughly 60/40 in favor of private boaters. Because commercial groups generally fill completely, the total numbers are closer to 50/50.

There is not much animosity on the Middle Fork between commercial and private floaters, though I personally have had a few confrontations with folks who don't support outfitting. If this is your opinion, please don't take in out on those who work for commercial operations. Write a letter to the Forest Service and other appropriate governing bodies.

Group Size and Organization
The number of people floating in private parties has grown due to the increased popularity of rafting, improved equipment, published articles (including this guidebook), and organized "permit parties" designed to improve the odds of drawing a permit. Consider the ramifications of floating with 20 to 24 people. It is the trip leader's responsibility to organize and manage the entire group. If you would rather float with fewer people, don't let outside pressures swell your numbers. Smaller parties are allowed longer trips and have greater flexibility to explore the canyon.

With the full compliment of twenty or more people, good communication and organization is vital to running a smooth and safe trip. Schedule a pre-trip "get acquainted" meeting to decide on the number of boats, discuss safety and rescue plans, and establish a trip leader who will manage the group and pass along river regulations and daily floating plans.

Number of Boats
There has also been an increase in the number of rafts per trip. I have seen a group of 16 people running 15 rafts and a kayak. The desire to row your boat the full 100 miles of the Middle Fork is understandable, but sharing the oars with others should be considered. I try to support 3 to 5 people per raft on private trips. Consider running a paddleboat with several bags strapped in the middle to increase your person to boat ratio.

Tappan Falls presents a low water challenge to a loaded sweep boat.

Lots of rafts create congestion at the put-in and take-out and spread over a longer stretch of river. This increases the visual and social impact along the corridor. A large party may fill an entire eddy at popular cultural or hiking stops.

The Forest Service does not regulate the number of boats per party. If you choose to have a large flotilla, organize and educate your group to reduce the social impacts on other floaters.

Slower Parties
Raft parties travel at different speeds. It is awkward and difficult to pass a group in mid-stream and results in raft congestion for several miles. There are as many as fifty parties spread over the 100 miles of river on a given day, so some overlap is inevitable. IT IS UP TO THE SLOWER PARTY to pull over and let a faster group pass. If your rafts pull out in front of an approaching party, accidentally or intentionally, make every effort to move downstream quickly and to create a buffer of space between the groups.

Sweep Boats
These large commercial cargo boats have a storied history on the Middle Fork and Main Salmon. They are unique to these river systems, so many floaters don't have experience running alongside this type of raft. Sweep Boats drift faster than the current and have no method of braking. When a Sweep boat approaches from behind please pull over and let it pass, especially when nearing rapids.

Solitude and Popular Sites
Many people float the Middle Fork to experience the solitude of a wilderness river. Nothing shatters this more than a loud, obnoxious party that pulls into the quiet hot spring you were enjoying. The crowded corridor along the Middle Fork is not a true "wilderness experience." There needs

to be give and take on both sides. If you have a rowdy group, quiet things down when passing other parties. On the other hand, be willing to accept some level of intrusion on your "wilderness experience."

There are many popular hikes and hot springs along the river. These are public resources and no one has proprietary rights. Accommodate other groups. Be courteous and polite. Share. Kindness and communication goes a long way. Trip leaders should generally avoid pulling in among another groups. Consider passing by a hot spring, choose an alternate landing (upstream of the mouth of Loon Creek for example), or continue on to an unoccupied site.

Cache Bar Take-Out

Cache Bar, like Boundary Creek, is a congested area where organization and cooperation are essential. The Forest Service has painted three un-loading zones on the downstream end of the ramp, but there is really only room for two parties to de-rig - one on each side of the ramp. When water levels permit, there is also room for two parties on the upstream side of the ramp. Some general "rules of the ramp:"

- STAY ORGANIZED by unloading gear into a single, narrow pile that leaves room for boats and cars. If your group is leaving in different vehicles, make piles appropriate for each car.
- UTILIZE everyone in the group to assist in the de-rig.
- Don't clog the concrete ramp with vehicles until ready to load the gear.
- MOVE QUICKLY. Try not hold others up. Everyone has a long day of travel ahead. Efficiency is appreciated.
- GANG DE-RIGGING one boat at a time is much more efficient than each person taking apart their own gear.
- COMMUNICATE your plan with other groups. Let them know you car may be on the ramp for 10 minutes, but you will move it as soon as you are finished.
- The ramp is for unloading and packing river gear. Move your personal bags to the top of the ramp,

A dirt ramp at the confluence with the Main Salmon is an alternative to the Cache Bar hustle and bustle. It is an option for a small group that doesn't want to run Cramer Creek Rapid. Communicating with other groups regarding take-out timetables helps everyone. Plan ahead for a stress free morning.

Using this Guide

The mile-by-mile descriptions provide detailed identification and technical information for running all significant rapids at all water levels. This guide covers many rapids and low water "shallows" that the current river map does not. Rapids that are significant only at low water are identified with red tick marks and text.

Clear, starry nights are frequent in mid summer.

In addition, camp descriptions, difficult pull-ins and important campsite notes are included. Historical and cultural points of interest, kayak play spots, photo opportunities, and over 130 hiking routes are noted on the maps. THE TEXT READS UP THE PAGE IN THE SAME DIRECTION THE RIVER FLOWS. Right and left always refers to the downstream "river right" or "river left" perspective. River mileage differs slightly from the old Forest Service map.

Maps

All the maps in this guide were created using National Geographic TOPO! CD-Rom software and provide detailed topographic information. The files were exported from the software in the 1:15,000 minute format and were resized slightly to fit the layout of this book. A scale bar and declination information are provided on the legend page.

All maps are oriented the same. North points up the page parallel to the spine of the book. Most of the original USGS base maps used a 40 foot contour interval, but some were printed with an 80 foot interval. These differences are "stitched" together in the seamless digital maps so pay attention to this discrepancy when planning hikes in the canyon.

 ## *Kayaking*
This guide identifies good surf waves or play holes for kayakers. At higher flows there are great surfing opportunities around nearly every bend. The kayak symbol identifies exceptional play features, mostly at moderate to low water. A more detailed description is included in the text.

There is ample opportunity for surfing along the way.

Hiking

The Middle Fork offers some of the best hiking opportunities of any river in the west. Though the river corridor can seem crowded at times, it only takes a short walk out of the social sphere of camp to regain that wilderness experience. Walking all or even a portion of the many hikes described in this book provides a very different perspective of the Middle Fork canyon.

Routes are marked with a red dashed line on the river maps and are labeled in reference to the camps from which they start. (ie. BC1 for Boundary Creek 1). Descriptions are found in the hiking section of the guide and include a quick summary of the class, mileage, and elevation gain to help estimate the time it may take to complete a route. A moderately fit hiker can climb approximately 1000 feet and/or 3 miles per hour.

The off-trail hikes generally follow ridgelines that are easy to identify and scout from the river and on the maps. The higher terrain provides spectacular views of the surrounding landscape.

I have hiked many of the routes in this guide. I also describe a few more from my personal to-do list. Routes I have not climbed that may present unknown challenges have a "?" after the class rating.

Hiking Classifications

- Class 1 - Hiking: There is a trail the entire way to the summit, though it may not be in great condition.
- Class 2 - Off-Trail Scrambling: These routes are off trail but you can probably walk to the summit, though occasionally using hands for balance but not to climb.
- Class 3 - Climbing: These routes involve actual climbing where arms and hands are used to ascend the slope. Class 3 climbing uses obvious holds involving minimal exposure, but a fall will hurt. Route finding skills are required.
- Class 4 - Belayed Climbing: These routes involve climbing that may be no more difficult than Class 3 but with increased exposure where a fall can cause serious injury. Training, proper equipment and precise route finding skills are essential.
- Class 5 - Belayed/Leader Protection: This is "technical" rock climbing pure and simple. Training and proper equipment are necessary.

Point-to-Point and Longer Routes

There are several "monster" hikes described in this book. If a member of your group is going to tackle one of these routes, consider a layover day to allow extra time. Another possibility is to plan a point-to-point hike, choosing appropriate camps and shuttling a boat to a pre-determined destination, allowing hikers ample time to complete the trek and finish at a waiting boat in day-light.

Safety Considerations

Many off-trail routes entail steep scrambling and require compass, map reading, and route finding skills. Extra clothing, food, water, compass, maps, and a headlamp are basic equipment for longer routes and point-to-point climbs.

Geology

The west's major rivers have carved deep chasms into its geologic underbelly, and many multi-day river trips float through the geologic past. The Middle Fork is no exception, and this guidebook includes a background of the regions geologic history. In addition, numerous geologic points of interest are noted on the maps with a geology hammer symbol. A description for each site follows the main geology text.

My personal background is in Geomorphology, the study of recent geologic landforms. I majored in geology at Middlebury College and conducted my thesis research on the Middle Fork with my advisor Grant Meyer. During the summers of 1995 and 1996 we studied the effects historical glaciations on the Middle Fork river system.

Since 1996, numerous landslides or "debris flows" have created new rapids and altered portions of the river corridor. This flurry of rare natural events has provided an interesting opportunity to observe geologic evolution first hand. The geology section focuses heavily on the Geomorphic history of the river canyon, and takes a close look at several of these recent "blow out" events. The photographs and observations presented in this guide provide a detailed history of recent events to reference as the river continues to evolve.

Photography

I have long searched for unique photographic perspectives of the Middle Fork landscape and have learned many tricks for shooting in the river environment. Unique opportunities are limited only by your imagination, and I have marked several photogenic locations on the maps with a camera symbol. A brief description is included in the appropriate mile-by-mile or hiking text.

Camera Equipment

My first camera in 1996 was a 35mm Canon SLR body with interchangeable lenses. The manual settings gave me creative control over the shutter speed and aperture settings, while automatic modes were useful for quick shots taken from the raft.

Variable zoom lenses are useful for river photography. The last thing a photographer wants to do on a moving boat is switch lenses while the composition slips by. Fixed focal length lenses do have better image quality, but my entire book "Impassable Canyon" was shot with a variable zoom lens.

I have used Tamron 28-200mm and 28-300mm zoom lenses since I started shooting. These light, compact lenses offer a wide range of compositional possibilities and are reasonable on the pocket book. Like most things in life,

There are many opportunities to capture white water images on the river.

however, you get what you pay for. These lenses are slower and less durable than more expensive models.

Storage and Protection

River photographers need to invest in a durable and waterproof plastic box such as those made by Pelican. A custom case to meet individual storage needs can be made by cutting out portions of the foam interior. Keep it simple. The constant in and out will eventually break down the foam divisions. Avoid intricate designs for each individual roll of film or battery. Instead, find a small, rectangular box (or make one out of cardboard and duct tape) to hold the little items and cut a space for it inside the case.

A solid, waterproof camera case is essential.

Pelican boxes are reliably waterproof for a couple of years and provide a bombproof housing for expensive equipment. I carry an over-the-shoulder soft case in my drybag for hiking trips, but otherwise the cameras stay in the Pelican. I have strapped the loaded Pelican to my lifejacket and swum the river, flipped boats with it strapped to the deck, and tossed it into plunge pools while negotiating side hikes in the Grand Canyon.

With of my knowledge of the river and over confidence in my skills, I keep my case untied and resting beneath the oarlock. This keeps it out of the range of the oar and protected from bouncing into the river (if it does, the box will float). When I see a photo opportunity, I just ship my oar, pop the lid closures, and I have two cameras ready to go.

For those less trusting of your own or your boat captain's rafting skills, leash the Pelican to the boat with a strap through the handle. This keeps your box tethered but allows quick access for opening the lid. I pre-rig a set of straps on my raft to lock the box firmly in place for big whitewater.

A Grand Canyon guidebook by Buzz Belknap offers some good advice: "lens caps only keep good pictures out." These little pieces of plastic are annoying, easily lost, and a hindrance to impromptu photos. I recommend screwing a neutral skylight filter onto your lens to protect the irreplaceable glass surface.

Sand will ruin a camera quicker than any other substance on a river trip. The safest place for your camera box is on the raft, especially on desert river trips. I hardly took my Pelican off the raft during my last Grand Canyon trip. Every time I washed my boat I doused the camera box to wash away fine sand that accumulates in the hinges and creases of the lid.

Always snap at least one lid closure shut. There is nothing worse than grabbing your camera case and spilling the entire contents into the river or sand because you forgot to lock the lid.

Tripod

A tripod is indispensable for creating fine art photographs or blurred water images. The cheap $30 to $50 dollar variety works just as well as the $600 lightweight carbon fiber model. Tiny tripods with flexible legs that stand just a few inches off the ground are useful for lightweight trips or belly-to-the-ground compositions.

This pink sky was balanced with a GND filter.

Filters

I use two filters. To cut glare, see into the crystal clear waters of the Middle Fork, or intensify the contrast of white clouds against a blue sky I use a circular polarizing filter. Polarizing filters darken the shadows of a composition, so I am selective in my application.

A filter that is vital when shooting a variably exposed composition is a Graduated Neutral Density filter or GND. These rectangular filters have from 1 to 3 stops of shading, and blend gradually across a piece of clear plastic or glass. The GND balances the exposure between a composition half in shadow and half lit by bright sun. The application is not immediately obvious in the canyon environment, but with compositional practice they are quite useful (see photo previous page).

It is worthwhile to purchase an expensive set of "Galen Rowell" GND filters from Singh Ray. The inexpensive plastic models offered by Kokin come with a cheap case and are easily scratched. I replace them on a regular basis. These filters work with the Kokin P-Filter system that attaches to the front of the lens. I have found that holding the filter flat against the lens with a steady hand works fine.

Wide Angle Lenses

I used to think that 28mm was wide enough until I bought a 17-85 variable zoom wide-angle lens. It increased my compositional options and the ability to capture more of the canyon landscape in a single, horizontal image. I highly recommend one of these for your river photography kit.

History

The native Shoshone Sheepeater or Tukuduka people, early white settlers, and pioneering rafters have left an extensive historical legacy in the Middle Fork canyon. Several historical points of interest are described in the mile-by-mile text, but there is more history than space available in these pages.

Cort Conley and Jim Carrey have done an invaluable service to the Middle Fork community through the research and printing of their excellent historical guidebook "The Middle Fork – A Guide." Their research was the only source I used while writing the historical points of interest in this book. Their book provides extensive detail of the American Indian, early white settlement, and rafting history of the Middle Fork. I highly recommended a copy for your river library.

When guiding the Middle fork, I like to remind my passengers of the contextual history in which the Tukuduka, white homesteaders, miners, and packers explored and lived along the canyon. The Sheepeater Indians lived for thousands of years on the flat benches along the river. Expert hunters, they enjoyed a comfortable existence subsisting off the wild animals and natural plants of the region. The discovery of gold and westward expansion brought many foreign white explorers to their their lands.

History was no different along the Middle Fork than the rest of the west, and the Tukuduka eventually lost their land to a more powerful white army during the "Sheepeater Wars" in 1878 and '79. The succession of white settlers and miners that followed were partially driven by the quest for gold. Many were hardy adventurers comfortable with carving a niche out of the remote canyon landscape. The west was still wild and population centers were few and far between, especially in central Idaho.

The second wave of Middle Fork inhabitants came to the wilderness to flee the depression. With little opportunity for work in the 1930's these settlers, predominately male, came to the river to fend for themselves. They lived off the land and whatever work they could find. Mining exploration in the region as well as trail cutting for the fledgling Forest Service augmented summertime gardens and subsistence hunting.

By the 1950's some of the homesteads and temporary cabins had been abandoned to begin a long battle with decay. Others changed hands enough times to interest wealthier owners and land speculators. Some of these properties eventually grew into the private in-holdings of land seen along the river (Pistol Creek Ranch, Middle Fork Lodge, Loon Creek Ranch, Tappan Ranch, and the Flying B to name a few).

Today, the year round population along the Middle Fork consists of little more than a few caretakers. A fraction of the number of American Indians and early white settlers that called the Middle Fork home during the previous thousand years.

River Flows

The Middle Fork is an un-dammed, natural river system with many large tributaries. Its waters are fed by melting snow from several distinct mountain ranges. The volume of the river is measured at two different gauges. The depth is taken from the bridge at the Middle Fork Lodge (mile 35) and a cubic foot per second (CFS) measurement is taken at the confluence with the Main Salmon (mile 96.2). Daily readings from both gauges are available from a USGS website (www.waterdata.usgs.gov/id/nwis/rt) The depth in feet from the M.F. Lodge is used throughout this guide.

Water levels will be highest from Mid-May to Mid-June. The peak can range from 4 to 10 feet depending on the winter snowpack. Keep in mind that many of the largest tributaries (Loon, Camas, Wilson, Waterfall, Ship Island, and Big Creek) add water below the M.F. Lodge. A reading taken at mile 35 will not always represent what is happening downstream below Big Creek (mile 78) in the Impassable Canyon.

The level can drop as low as 1.2 feet in a drought year, but averages 1.75 feet on the first of September. The USGS website provides the following conversion from feet to CFS. Refer to the graphs below showing selected summer flows and the cooresponding winter snowpack data.

Feet	CFS
1	183
1.5	430
2	845
2.5	1,360
3	1,960
3.5	2,690
4	3,540
4.5	4,400

Feet	CFS
5	5,330
5.5	6,340
6	7,640
6.5	8,760
7	10,200
8	13,600
8.3	14,600
10.8(1974)	20,900

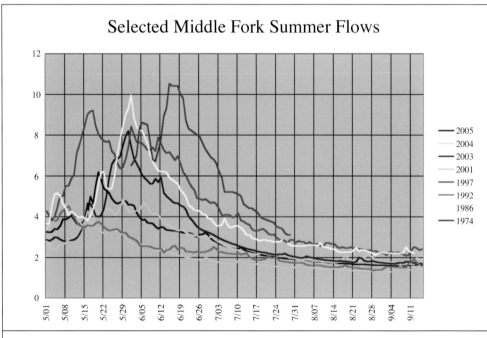

Selected Middle Fork Summer Flows

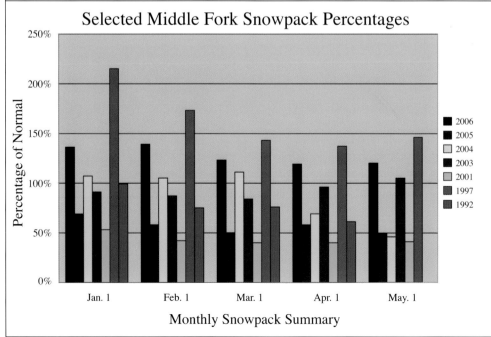

Selected Middle Fork Snowpack Percentages

River Maps

The remainder of this guide is divided into three sections: River Maps, Hiking, and Geology. While the maps provide complete visual information, textual descriptions for the hikes and geologic points of interest are included in the Hiking and Geology sections that follow. A traditional legend is included on the first map page, and the diagram to the right helps understand how to read the river maps.

The Middle Fork flows in a northerly direction over its entire course. The maps are orientated north (up the spine of the book) so the river flows up the pages. The reader will quickly notice that the text associated with each river map also reads up the page. Once accustomed to this format, I believe it is much easier to keep track of your location as you float through the corridor.

In order to limit the mile-by-mile text to a single page per map, the descriptions are limited to high and low water rapids, kayak play spots, riverside camps, and various points-of-interest along the corridor. Mileage is marked starting from Boundary Creek (mile 0) and arrows indicate the direction of river flow.

In addition, water spigot symbols show locations where potable water is available. Boundary Creek, Indian Creek and the Flying B Ranch provide filtered or treated water. The other sources are natural, untreated springs or creeks that commercial outfitters have used for years. The photographs included on each page generally relate to something along that section of the river corridor.

Organizing this guide into a user-friendly format has been a challenging and rewarding project. Input from individuals along the way helped shaped the look and feel of the layout. I sincerely hope the information provided with these maps and guide maximizes your safety and enjoyment while floating the Middle Fork of the Salmon River. Have fun!

Notes

The **mileage** from Boundary Creek (mile 0) is labeled in one mile increments all the way to Cache Bar (mile 98.9). The mileage differs slightly from the existing Forest Service map.

The **camera symbol** highlights particularly scenic locations on many of the hikes. Good whitewater and riverside photo opportunities are noted as well.

There are 73 **Geologic points-of-interest** labeled with a grey text box on the maps. Each is assigned a number beginning with G1 at Sulphur Creek near the top of the river. The tip of the geology hammers point to a specific rock or landform. Detailed descriptions for each hammer begin on page 85 after the main geologic text.

Historical, **cultural**, and other **points-of-interest** are marked with a purple dot and cooresponding text box. A description of each site is included in the mile-by-mile text.

Low water rapids are identified by red tick marks across the river and red text in the box. A description is included on the opposite page

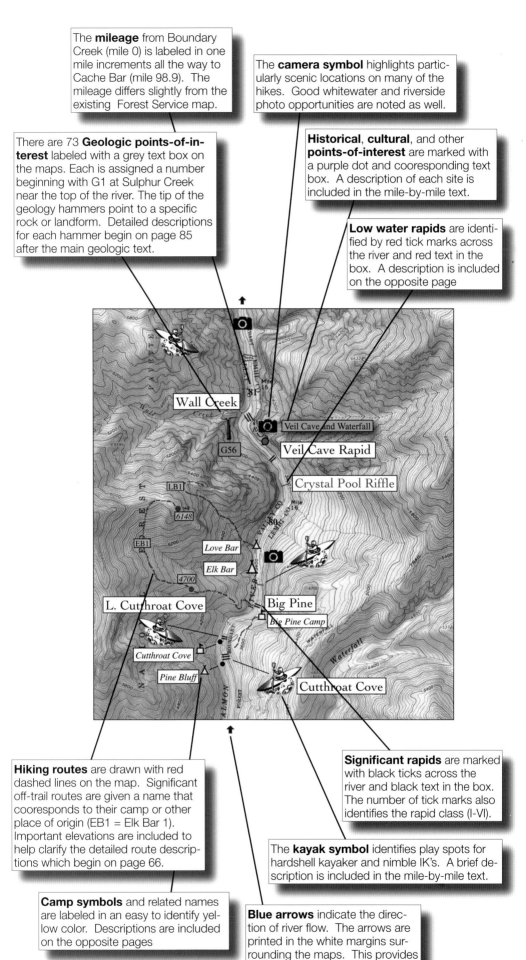

Hiking routes are drawn with red dashed lines on the map. Significant off-trail routes are given a name that cooresponds to their camp or other place of origin (EB1 = Elk Bar 1). Important elevations are included to help clarify the detailed route descriptions which begin on page 66.

Significant rapids are marked with black ticks across the river and black text in the box. The number of tick marks also identifies the rapid class (I-VI).

The **kayak symbol** identifies play spots for hardshell kayaker and nimble IK's. A brief description is included in the mile-by-mile text.

Camp symbols and related names are labeled in an easy to identify yellow color. Descriptions are included on the opposite pages

Blue arrows indicate the direction of river flow. The arrows are printed in the white margins surrounding the maps. This provides a quick visual reference for the reader.

Mile By Mile Descriptions

<u>Mile 3.2 - Sulphur Slide Rapid (1st Slide Rapid):</u> Two 90 degree turns below Pinball empty into a large pool above this rapid. Pull over on the left bank above several dead tree stumps to scout. The rapid was formed by a landslide from river right in 1936. (see G4 on page 85).
High Water: (Class III) It's a bumpy straightforward run with lots of waves and holes at high water. Watch out for a large wrap rock left of center at the top.
Low Water: (Class III+) This rapid is notoriously tricky at flows below 2.5 feet. The recommended entrance is along the left bank. Carry good speed out of the pool and ship your left oar to avoid scraping the bank. Pass the large wrap rock on the left before working back towards the center. Run left of center in the lower section. The many large angular landslide boulders often require switching to plan B and sometimes C, D, or F. Use proper spacing.

Mile 2.9 - Gardells Hole: (634892E 4936202N). This small gravel bar/beach camp is located on the upstream end of the Sulphur Slide pool. It will be very small or washed out at higher flows.

<u>Mile 2.5 - Pinball Rapid - Low Water:</u> (Class III) A calm straightaway below the mouth of Sulphur Creek will end in a deep pool with an avalanche path on river right. Carry good speed out of the pool and work from center to left downstream. Slow down and look for a narrow channel that sneaks between dry boulders along the left bank. Work back to center below this slot. Use proper spacing. THIS IS THE ONLY LOW WATER CHANNEL.

Mile 2 – Sulphur Creek and Morgan Ranch: In 1904, Jim and Annazie Fuller homesteaded land a quarter mile up the creek. They trailed cattle downstream from Bruce Meadows and summered with their five children on the ranch. Later, they sold the place to Dr. Ben Morgan. The airstrip that provides access to the Morgan Ranch was cleared in the late 40's.

<u>Mile 1.8 - Doors Rock:</u> About a half mile below Teepee Hole the river swings right and points directly at a steep slope of talus and cliff outcrops before turning abruptly back left. Doors Rock is directly underneath these cliffs.
High Water: Water piles into the sheer right bank to form powerful boils and eddies. Aim for the downstream end of these boils and slip between the wall and Doors Rock/hole in the center. I recommend this line until 3 feet. Pulling left of the rock exposes a raft to a wrap hazard that is greatest between 3 and 5.5 feet.
Low Water: Run the boulder strewn entrance right. Wait for deeper water before pulling left of Door's Rock. Get ready to work right immediately below the rock because drifting left will maroon your boat on a sharp bedrock shelf.

Mile 1.8 - Point of Interest - Snowstorm Cabin: Pull over on the right bank upstream of Doors Rock. Wander downstream towards the rocky talus hillside to find a cabin nestled among an aspen grove. The roof is collapsed, but a stone fireplace and walls remain. If time allows, explore along the base of the hill in search of the Snowstorm mine shaft and more cabins further east.

The hard rock Snowstorm mine had been worked prior to the official claim filed by Leo Dodge, Joe Fox, and Homer Granger in 1927. The partners split in 1930. Leo kept the Snowstorm mine and gave Joe rights to the claim downstream at Little Soldier Creek. Joe placer mined the Little Soldier claim with Leo's son Rosco. Leo and his wife Emily used the Snowstorm cabins for more than 20 years. Dr. Ben Morgan from across the river at Sulphur Creek bought the claim in 1950 for $6000. He wanted the land to graze his horses.

Mile 1.7 - Cable Hole Camp: (635116E 4934572N) A small obscure camp on river left above Doors Rock.

Mile 1 Teepe Hole Camp: (635551E 4933761N) A small camp located on the left side of a deep pool below Murph's Hole. This is a good spot to regroup after the first fast-moving mile of water.

<u>Mile .9 - Murph's Hole - High Water:</u> (Class IV) Watch for the first 90 degree left hand turn on the river. A large rock forms Murph's Hole at the peak of this turn. Run a small rapid on the right bank just upstream before setting up to run Murph's Hole. This powerful hydraulic has flipped a fully loaded sweep boat. There are three possible runs. #1 is to pull hard across the current river left of the hole. Don't bounce off the left hand gravel bar back into the hole. #2 is to center punch the hole and hope for the best. #3 is the run I recommend. Forward push to the outside of the bend and sneak the hole along the right bank. Below 4 feet Murph's Hole loses its punch.

<u>Mile .1 - First Bend Rapid:</u> You can see this rapid from the boat launch. There is a long stretch of class III water downstream.
High Water: (Class III+) Run either the center or right channel. The river below moves quickly through narrow bedrock channels. There are no large holes, but expect swift currents and large waves. Back pulling is recommended through this fast moving section.
Low Water: (Class III) Run center. Be ready for narrow channels with little space to maneuver downstream. Ship your oars as necessary. Use proper spacing as a pile up here can be nasty.

<u>Mile 0 - Boundary Creek Campground and Boat Launch:</u> (635554E 4932305N) Fill out permits, register for camps, top off your water jugs, and receive your Forest Service talk here. Keep your required items available for inspection. Please take only four spaces along the shore in the eddy and tie the rest of your boats off the end of these rafts.

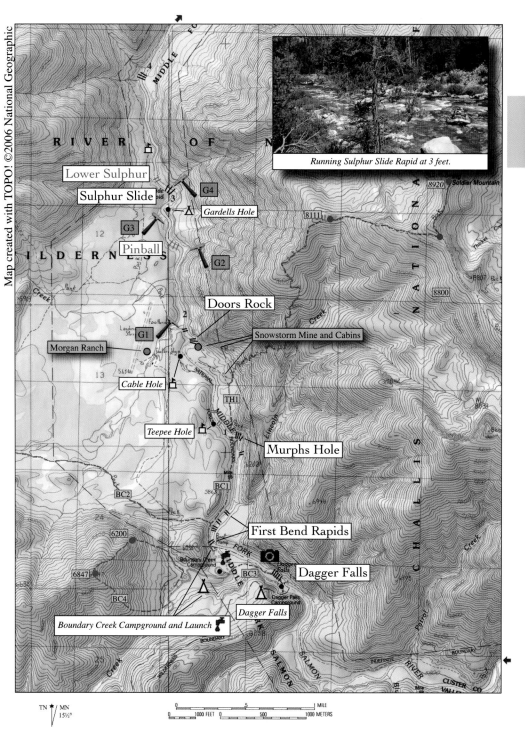

Running Sulphur Slide Rapid at 3 feet.

Lower Sulphur
Sulphur Slide
G4
Gardells Hole
G3
Pinball
G2
Doors Rock
Snowstorm Mine and Cabins
G1
Morgan Ranch
Cable Hole
TH1
Teepee Hole
Murphs Hole
BC1
BC2
First Bend Rapids
BC3
Dagger Falls
6200
6847
BC4
Boundary Creek Campground and Launch
Dagger Falls

TN / MN
15½°

0   5   1 MILE
0   1000 FEET   0   500   1000 METERS

Legend

(This legend applies to all the river maps)

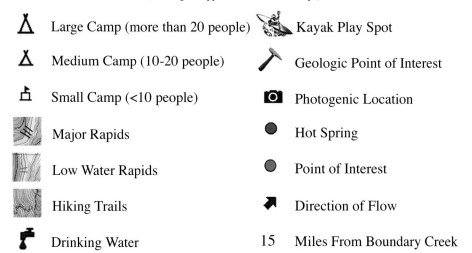

Large Camp (more than 20 people)   Kayak Play Spot

Medium Camp (10-20 people)   Geologic Point of Interest

Small Camp (<10 people)   Photogenic Location

Major Rapids   Hot Spring

Low Water Rapids   Point of Interest

Hiking Trails   Direction of Flow

Drinking Water   15   Miles From Boundary Creek

25

Map created with TOPO! ©2006 National Geographic

Mile 8.1 - Lower Chutes: (Class II+) This is another frustrating low water spot with no clear channel along the right side of the river. Leave the pool with speed, working from center to right of center. Push hard over some large submerged boulders and pick a left, right, left line through the rock garden downstream.

Mile 7.9 - Chutes Rapid (Snow Hole): Two large avalanche chutes drop into the right hand side of a 90 degree left hand turn. There is a wide, calm section at the apex of the turn. The Chutes begin below.
High Water: (Class III) Pass right of a large wrap rock/hole left of center at the top. A fun bouncy ride with no difficult moves follows downstream.
Low Water: (Class III+) Below 2.5 feet this rapid becomes very tricky. Carry speed out of the pool right of center and work left of the big wrap rock (but not too soon). Once below the rock move immediately into the right channel and follow it over several more drops to the pool below. If you miss this first right cut, bide your time left for one more drop before cutting back right for the finish. At extremely low flows squeeze right of the big rock at the top to access the right channel downstream. Use proper spacing.

Mile 7.7 - Upper Chutes #1 and #2: Below 2 feet the riffles encountered below Trail Flat hot springs become bad sticky spots. In #1 DON'T get suckered into the right or left hand channel. Carry speed into the riffle left of center and work to finish left at the bottom. In #2 pass the large rock on the right and work left below.

Mile 7.3 - Trail Flat Camp: (637320E 4940957N) This camp is located on a high bench about 50 feet above the river. The hot spring is under water at flows above 4.5 feet. The upstream pull-in facilitates an easier carry.

Mile 6.8 - Big Bend Camp: (636572E 4941224N) A beautiful camp with a large sandbar on the inside of a sharp right hand turn. Great kayak surfing forms in the wave train on the outside of the bend at flows above 5 feet.

Mile 5.7 - Boy Scout Camp: (635830E 4939894N) This medium-sized sand bar is easy to miss because it is invisible from upstream. Look for a rocky pull-in on the right bank in the straight-away below Velvet Falls.

Mile 5.3 - Velvet Falls: Below the HHM gorge, Spike Creek enters from river left below a bedrock outcrop. Scout from this eddy via a 1/8 mile rafters trail leading downstream. Around the corner look for a huge triangular boulder on river left opposite the cascading Velvet Creek on river right. The Falls span the entire river between these two features. Photo opportunities are availble from the scout, or by pulling in to the right bank eddy below the rapid. Scramble up the bank for a perspective above the rapid.
High Water: (Class IV) At flows above 6.5 to 7 feet a sneak forms left of the big triangular rock, otherwise forward push a 16 to 18 foot oar boat over the drop through a fluctuating weakness right of center (until about 4 feet). To avoid the hole, push or pull into the powerful eddy below the triangular rock and use the swirling current to swing your boat just left of the main hole. The timing for this move is tricky. Pull too soon and you bounce off the triangular rock into the meat of Velvet Falls, too late and you're also a goner. Good luck! Set up safety from the scout, as well as the eddy on river right below the falls.
Low Water: (Class II+) Catch the eddy below the triangular rock and remember to ship your left oar forward as you run the stair-step drop along the left bank.

Mile 4.7 - Hells Half Mile (2nd Slide Rapid): A half mile of straight, calm water below Rams-horn Rapid leads to a shady left hand turn with a small creek tumbling in on river right.
High Water: (Class III+) Above 4 feet skirt the wide bumpy entrance inside left. The river narrows quickly to the left of a gravel island and enters a small bedrock gorge punctuated by large holes on both sides of the river. Be ready for anything in this fast moving half mile.
Low Water: (Class III) The entrance to HHM is sticky at low water. A right of center run is open until about 2 feet. Below 2 feet look for a narrow, dead-end slot between dry boulders left of center. Drift slowly into this slot and then pull back into the right of center run. Work left below the entrance. Watch out for the submerged bedrock boulder at the base of the left wall as you rocket into the gorge. Use proper spacing.

Mile 4 - Ramshorn Rapid: (Class III) Look for a large bedrock outcrop on the river left bank .75 miles below Sulphur Slide. A small creek pours into the eddy below this rock. Run Ramshorn left of center. At high water get ready to pull off the wall on bottom left, or at least hit it straight on with the nose of your boat. At lower flows watch out for the smooth, black wrap rock right of center. The morning view downstream from this rapid is sublime for photographers.

Mile 3.4 - Spring Camp: (634737E 4936862N) A fast pull-in to a small grassy camp below Sulphur Creek Rapid.

Mile 3.3 - Lower Sulphur Rapid: (Class II+) Drift left at the entrance to this low water rapid to avoid shallow gravels at the top. Pull hard right to avoid a sticky bedrock ledge in the center below.

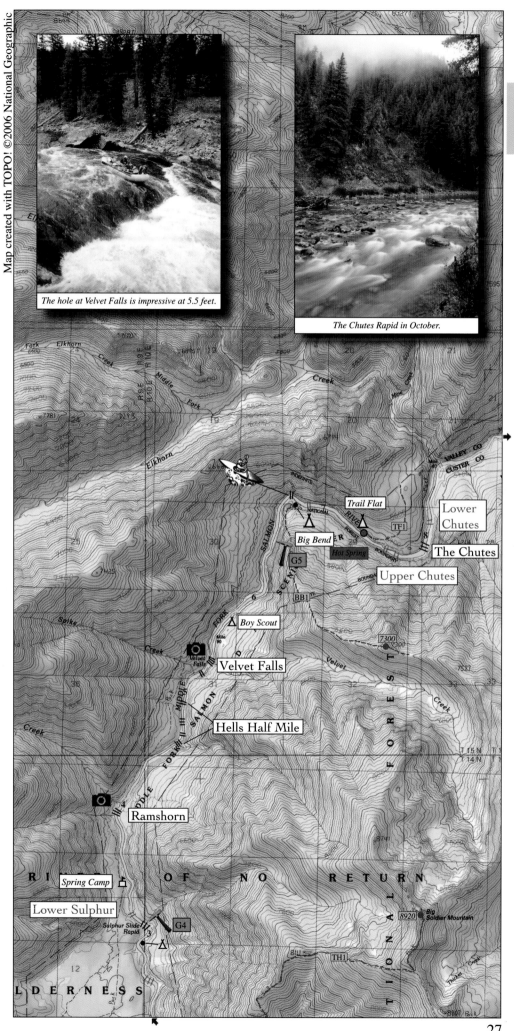

The hole at Velvet Falls is impressive at 5.5 feet.

The Chutes Rapid in October.

Lower
Chutes

The Chutes

Upper Chutes

Trail Flat

TF1

Big Bend

Hot Spring

G5

Boy Scout

Velvet
Falls

Velvet Falls

Hells Half Mile

Ramshorn

RI   O F   N O   R E T U R N

Spring Camp

Lower Sulphur

Sulphur Slide
Rapid

G4

Big
Soldier Mountain

TH1

L D E R N E S S

27

Mile 13.1 - Scout Camp: (642853E 4942826N) At the apex of the Sheepeater bend is a small camp on the left bank. Sandy tent sites can be found nestled among the trees.

Mile 13 - Sheepeater Shallows: At flows below 2 feet stay on the outside of the entrance to Sheepeater bend.

Mile 12.5 - Sheepeater Island: A large bedrock island with trees on top splits the river left of center. Watch for high water logs broached on the upstream side of the island. Run left at low water.

Mile 12.1 - Point of interest - Joe Bump Cabin: Walk upstream from the camp along the forested bench to visit another historical mining cabin. In the 1930's Roscoe Dodge worked a placer claim here with his father-in-law, Joe Fox. They built the cabin and dug a long diversion ditch and wing dam to divert water to their claim further down the bar. The effort was "a starve-out affair" recalled Dodge, and very little gold was recovered from the effort. Piles of placer-worked gravel can be found along the left bank downstream.

Joe Bump, a prospecting friend of Fox and Dodge, added the front entry to the cabin. In later years Elmer "Settrigger" Purcell, another miner who worked and lived in Middle Fork region, migrated to the Bump cabin and eventually died of an apparent heart attack. His grave maker, several hundred yards downstream near the original placer claim, was erected in 1976.

Mile 12.1 - Joe Bump Camp: (641729E 4942937N) Skirt Soldier Ceek Rapid on the inside left to catch a small eddy. The camp is located on the bench above the river. If you miss the eddy, there is an alternate pull-in downstream above some small cliffs on river left. The bench is rich in mining history.

Mile 12.1 – Soldier Creek Rapid: The first sharp right hand turn below Powerhouse has a small rapid at the mouth of Soldier Creek. Look for some low water kayak surf waves here. A man by the name of Bill Brockman operated a hard rock gold mine several miles up Soldier Creek. He and his crew bored a tunnel nearly 300 feet into the mountainside in search of the precious ore.

Mile 11.5 - Powerhouse Rapid (Waterwheel Rapid): The fire scars on river right and broad talus slopes remind me of the approaching rapids just over a mile downstream. Scout from the cabin and ore stamp trail. The rapid is named for the waterwheel built on the right bank. I break Powerhouse into three sections. Upper Powerhouse runs past the historic ore stamp on river right. The middle section follows a long s-turn that crashes into a cliff wall at the bottom right. Lower Powerhouse continues downstream from the wall.
Upper Powerhouse – (Class III) This straight section passes the old waterwheel on river right. Run left of center past several holes and boulders. This is followed by a brief pool.
Middle Powerhouse High Water – (Class IV) The river makes a right hand turn and follows a fast and bumpy run along a steep river bank. On the next left turn, run inside of a large boulder hole. Continue working left through big waves and holes for a final pull to avoid the wall on the bottom right.
Middle Powerhouse Low Water – (Class III+) Around 3 feet a "Shark Rock" comes out at the end of the straight section along the left bank. It is hard to pick out, but pass it on the right. Run inside of the boulder-hole on the left turn below. Low water forces you further right before pulling left off the wall at the bottom. Use proper spacing. Take a breather or have lunch at the bottom. It is fun to swim into the micro eddies against the wall at low flows. It is a great place to play with river hydrauics in a relatively safe setting.
Lower Powerhouse High Water – (Class III) At high flows, the rapid continues downstream towards a dangerous chunk of bedrock left of center. High water logs sometimes span the left channel. Run right of this significant wrap hazard.

Mile 11.3 - Point of Interest - Powerhouse Cabin and Ore Stamp: Look for a trail leaving a low grassy bench (below 3 feet) on river right downstream from a small cliff wall. You can scout Upper Powerhouse Rapid from here.

The cabin on the bench above Upper Powerhouse Rapid served as seasonal housing for miners working the White Goat claim across the river. They wintered at Sheepeater Hot Springs downstream. They sank a vertical shaft into the mountain and packed the ore by mule to a cable strung across the river. Sam Sibbitts built the water-driven ore stamp for Charlie Smith and Gene Hussey, who established the claim. Fred Paulson worked the mine for a while in the thirties but abandoned the unprofitable venture. Outfitters shuttled several batches of shingles to the site in 1991 when the Forest Service re-roofed the cabin and replaced several logs in the decaying structures.

Mile 9.9 - Boot Camp: (640171E 4942278N) A small camp located on a high timbered bench around the corner from Saddle Camp.

Mile 9.7 - Saddle Camp: (639955E 4942464N) Look for a large grassy saddle high above the river on the left bank. The camp is located on a treed bench above the river.

Mile 9 - Rapid Camp: (638999E 4942063N) A small camp across the river and downstream from Elkhorn Bar Camp.

Mile 8.9 - Elkhorn Bar Camp: (638876E 4941968N) Pass Elkhorn Creek and look for a small waterfall among the trees on the right bank. Not far below is a large boulder in the center of the river. Pull in on the right bank below the bolder to access this broad timbered bench.

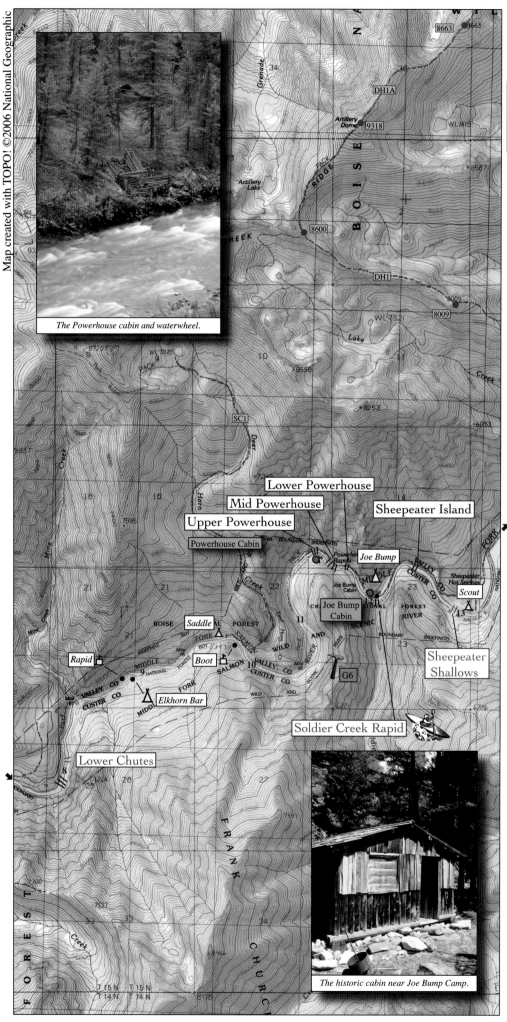

The Powerhouse cabin and waterwheel.

Lower Powerhouse

Mid Powerhouse

Upper Powerhouse

Powerhouse Cabin

Sheepeater Island

Joe Bump

Scout

Joe Bump Cabin

Saddle

Rapid

Boot

Sheepeater Shallows

Elkhorn Bar

G6

Soldier Creek Rapid

Lower Chutes

The historic cabin near Joe Bump Camp.

29

Mile 17.7 - Artillery Rapid #3: Follow a short straightaway below #2 into a slight left hand turn. There is a chunk of bedrock that sits right of center on the turn.

High Water – (Class II) Above 6 feet the bedrock chunk will be mostly submerged. The right channel can clog with high water logs so stay left. Downstream, work left of the large hole/pour-over in the center.

Low Water - (Class II+) Run just left of the bedrock boulder. Sweep boat drivers should beware of damaging their cowling on this rock. Run left of the second boulder downstream. Catch the eddy and pull hard right immediately below for the cleanest channel. This is a common sticky spot in low water.

Mile 17.6 - Artillery Boulder Garden: A low water rock dodge between #2 and #3.

Mile 17.5 - Artillery Rapid #2: Located on the second right hand bend in the series, this is a fun rapid at high water.

Low Water - (Class II+) Enter left. Drift longer than you think past the shallow boulders in the center, before pulling hard to the right of a large dry boulder. THERE IS NO RIGHT CHANNEL BELOW 2 FEET. Use proper spacing.

Mile 17.3 - Artillery Ledge Hole: (Class III) Follow the straightaway below Artillery #1 until the river bends to the left. At flows in the 5 foot range a large bedrock ledge hole develops on river right. Avoid or have fun with this feature.

Mile 16.9 - Artillery Rapid #1: The 3/4 mile straightaway below Greyhound Creek ends in a gentle turn to the left.

High Water – (Class II+) This marks the beginning of a mile and a half of relatively continuous class II and III water with highlights at the marked rapids. Run left of center.

Low Water – (Class II+) The tricky low water begins upstream of the rapid. Run left of center as the river shallows (just right of Snowmobile Rock) and pick a line downstream from there. Hug inside right of a white bedrock shelf on the sharp turn below. Run the main rapid left of center through boulders.

Mile 16.7 – Point of Interest - Mortar Creek Fire Re-growth: Recovery from the Mortar Creek Fire is apparent along the right bank. It has taken over 27 years for new trees to grow on the flat benches and north facing slopes along the right bank. With present day climate change, some slopes may never grow back into the thick forests that existed prior to the burn. Photographs showing this regrowth offer a nice perspective on the recovery.

Mile 16.1 - Dome Hole Camp: (645400E 4945761N). Float through the Greyhound Pool and pull in on the left bank downstream to access this small camp. The 1979 Mortar Creek Fire started downstream. Three horse campers neglected to properly extinguish their campfire. It smoldered in the dangerously dry conditions before exploding out of control. The fire raged until August 11th, 1979 burning nearly 64,000 acres along 20 miles of the Middle Fork corridor.

Mile 16 - Greyhound Camp S-turns and Boil: (Class II) There is a small rapid at the base of the cliff across from camp. Kayakers may find some fun surfing possibilities at medium flows. Below the pool, the river boils off a sloping bedrock wall on river right. Skilled rafters can have fun playing with the recoiling boil while novice boaters should hug the left bank. The boil pours into a good sized, surfable ledge hole forms between 2.5 and 5 feet of water. Watch for IK swims.

Mile 16 - Greyhound Camp: (645347E 4945711N) Stay inside right below Greyhound Creek and pull in to the eddy across from a small rapid and cliff wall. There is a small treed bench that is tight for a large group. A man named Hale worked a placer claim on the bench. The foundation of his cabins and mining gravels can still be found among placer-worked gravels.

Mile 15.3 - Johns Camp: (644476E 4945198N) Turn the corner below Lake Creek Camp and pull in to a narrow sand bar along the rocky shore.

Mile 14.9 - Lake Creek Camp: (644298E 4944917N) Pull in to a rocky shoreline on river right directly across from Lake Creek. A hot spring bubbles up in the rocks along the river, but is underwater at flows above 4 feet.

Mile 14.8 - Lake Creek Shallows: Below 2 feet carry as much speed as possible into this wide, shallow gravel bar. Keep pushing all the way through.

Mile 14.5 - Fire Island Shallows: After rounding the first left turn below Fire Island, work to the inside left bank to find the deepest water.

Mile 13.9 - Fire Island Camp: (643238E 4943828N) Pull in just upstream of a small bedrock island on the left bank. A large downed tree along the bank will complicate this landing. The camp is named for the hot spring that emerges under water at the base of the bedrock island. Keep your bug spray handy as there is some standing water behind camp.

Mile 13.3 - Sheepeater Camp: (643015E 4943106N) There is an upstream pull-in among several trees (high to medium flows) or swift pull-in to a gravel bank on the downstream end of the bar. A large, grassy flat accommodates many tents. Follow one of the several trails to the hot springs which emerge from the hillside surrounded by a boulder studded mud flat. Powerhouse miners Smith and Hussey built two winter cabins at this site as well as a bath house over one of the hot springs on the flat. Only a few decaying logs remain. Deer and elk are attracted to the natural minerals in the hot water. I once enjoyed an hour watching a family of mountain goats drink from the springs.

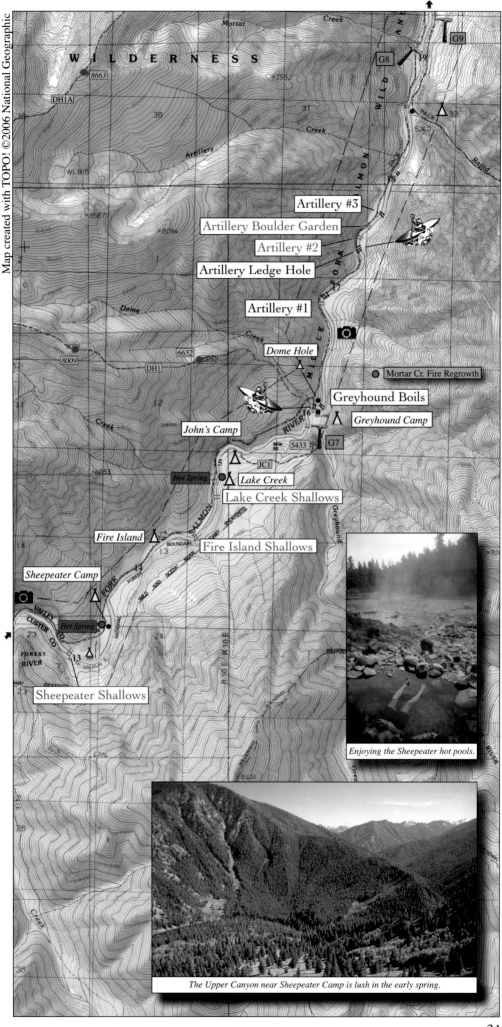

WILDERNESS

DH1A

Artillery #3

Artillery Boulder Garden

Artillery #2

Artillery Ledge Hole

Artillery #1

Dome Hole

Mortar Cr. Fire Regrowth

Greyhound Boils

Greyhound Camp

John's Camp

DH1

Hot Spring

Lake Creek

Lake Creek Shallows

Fire Island

Fire Island Shallows

Sheepeater Camp

Hot Spring

Sheepeater Shallows

G9

G8

G7

JC1

5433

Enjoying the Sheepeater hot pools.

The Upper Canyon near Sheepeater Camp is lush in the early spring.

Mile 21.9 - Point of Interest – Huntington Claim and Mining Dredge: Pull in to a small sand bar after turning the corner below Lake Creek Rapid. A decaying bucket dredge once stood at a pile of gravel tailings. It has since fallen over.

Ed Huntington and his partners diverted water from Lake Creek upstream. They hand bored several pieces of 10 foot wooden pipe before using a gas powered engine to finish the task. Over 1200 feet of wire-wrapped wooden pipe brought pressurized water from their Lake Creek diversion. They used this water to power the bucket dredge and placer mine for gold in the river deposits along the bar.

The mining operation was funded by investors from the East Coast. It never panned out, and Huntington fled to South America after mismanaging the investment monies.

Mile 21.8 - Point of Interest - Huntington Cabin: Before the Lake Creek slide altered the river, there was a easy gravel bar pull-in on the left bank to access the old Huntington Cabin. Boaters should probably pull in on the left bank upstream of the debris fan/rapid and walk down to the cabin. I have not visited the site since 2000 and do not know if the cabin was destroyed in the fires.

Ed Huntington, R.M. Teachout, and E. S. Pickhardt filed a 20 acre mining claim upstream of Pistol Creek on October 18, 1938. They built the cabin and a bridge across the river over Pistol Creek Rapids to access their placer mining operations. The concrete foundations for the bridge can be found on the cliffs just upstream of the main rapid.

Mile 21.7 - Quick Stop Camp: (647153E 4953520N) A small camp used to exist below the bedrock outcrop at the downstream end of the Lake Creek fan. The old camp is buried by the Lake Creek debris.

Mile 21.7 - Lake Creek Rapid: (Class II+) The long straightaway below Cannon Creek ends on a gentle left turn. A large debris fan pours in from river right. This landslide rapid is evolving, but the run is along the left bank. At low water stay left through the shallows below.

On August 11th, 2000 our river crew weathered a large thunderstorm at Cradle Creek Camp down in Impassable Canyon that rained lightning bolts onto the mountains along the Middle Fork. That storm system started over 35 individual fires within the Middle Fork drainage. On August 16th the Forest Service closed the river to all float boat traffic because of fire danger.

The Little Pistol Creek fire roared across the Middle Fork on August 26th and burned up the flanks of Little Soldier Mtn. It destroyed 17 cabins downstream at the Pistol Creek Ranch. The following summer, an August thunderstorm drenched the fire-denuded slopes of Lake Creek resulting in the major debris-flow that created this new rapid.

Mile 20 - Cannon Creek Rapid (3rd Slide): Below Dolly Lake camp is a remnant landslide rapid.
High Water - (Class III-) At very high flows (above 7 feet) the right side of Cannon Creek forms a huge hole. Read and run at high water and float either side of the logjam island downstream.
Low Water – (Class II+) Starting around 3.5 feet a ledge hole forms on the bottom right for good paddle boat and kayak surfing. Stay left to avoid the hole. Run left of the logjam island downstream.

Mile 19.8 - Dolly Lake Camp: (646579E 4950889N) Look for two large dead Ponderosa trees on the right bank downstream of Dolly Lake. Pull in between these trees. Several tent sites are scattered among the bushes.

Mile 19.7 - Big Snag Camp: (646800E 4950725N) A small gravel bar looks over Dolly Lake from the left bank. Climb to the upper benches for more tent sites. The "Big Snag" and "Dolly Lake" camp names were inadvertently switched long ago. I kept the same names to avoid confusion with the Forest Services camp reservation system.

Mile 18.9 - Mortar Creek Island: There is a nice fishing pool and underwater bedrock canyon upstream of this island. Take the right channel at low water. You can fill your water bottle from a small spring on the right bank upstream of the pool.

Mile 18.5 - Rapid River Riffle: (Class II) This is a fun bedrock wave train on a small right hand turn below Rapid River.

Mile 18.5 - Rapid River Camp: (646403E 4949125N) Hard to access at low water, this site sits on a large timbered bench just downstream from the mouth of Rapid River. The pull-in is fast at high water. Rapid River is one of a handful of Middle Fork tributaries that sees occasional kayak descents.

Mile 18.1 - Artillery Rapid #4: (Class II-) A fun and easy wave train with a small cliff outcrop on river right.

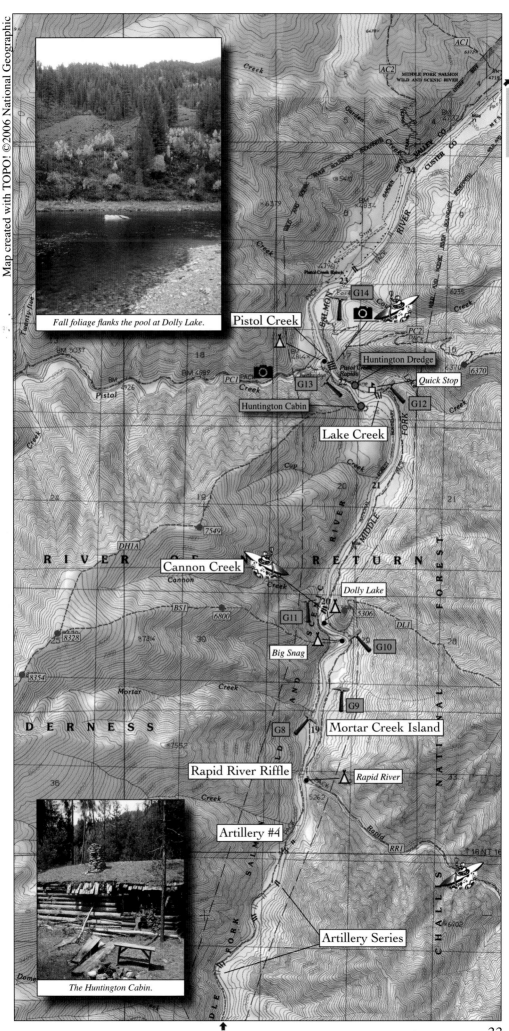

Fall foliage flanks the pool at Dolly Lake.

Pistol Creek

G14

Huntington Dredge

PC2

Quick Stop

PC1

G13

Huntington Cabin

G12

Lake Creek

7549

DH1A

Cannon Creek

Dolly Lake

BS1

6800

G11

DL1

Big Snag

G10

8328

8354

G9

Mortar Creek Island

G8

Rapid River Riffle

Rapid River

Artillery #4

RR1

The Huntington Cabin.

Artillery Series

33

Mile 27 - Indian Creek Camp: (651054E 4959097N) There is a swift pull-in just upstream of Indian Creek. The camp is perched on the peninsula between the Middle Fork and Indian Creek.

Mile 26.3 - Indian Creek Pack Bridge: This bridge connects the Rapid River trail system with the main Middle Fork Trail on river left.

Mile 25.7 - Indian Creek Shallows: The river is wide and shallow for nearly a mile below Indian Creek Launch. Expect slow going below 2 feet. Stay left when you leave the launch and right when passing underneath the pack bridge downstream.

Mile 25.5 – Indian Creek Guard Station and Camp: (649280E 4957703N). The large beach is covered with high water logs, but has ample room for several groups. The airstrip and launch ramp are used at very high and very low water to avoid the upper 25 miles of river. Early and late season trips that launch when Boundary Creek is closed must check in here with the ranger for their permit and camp assignments.

   The bench above the river was first occupied by Eleck and Martha Watson who also lived upstream in Sam Hopkin's cabin at Pistol Creek. Their grandchildren, Fred Paulson and Daisy Tappan, were the only kids growing up in the canyon and the time. They both would return to lives along the Middle Fork.

Mile 25.5 - Indian Creek Launch Rapid: (Class II-) This small class II rapid has some kayak surfing to play in at various levels.

Mile 24.9 - Airplane Camp: (648676E 4957157N) Pull in below a small left turn upstream of a large gravel and grass island. Carry your camp 20 feet up the left bank to a flat grassy bench among large Ponderosa trees.

Mile 23.3 - Pistol Cabins Shallows: There are two wide shallows below the kayak ledge surfing upstream. Stay right on the first one, and left on the second.

Mile 23 - Pistol Cabins Ledge: After passing several of the Pistol Creek cabins, the river makes a sharp turn to the right. A long bedrock ledge forms a fun hydraulic. Kayaks and paddleboats will find good eddy-feed-surfing starting at 4 feet. Run inside right to avoid the ledge.

Mile 22.8 - Point of Interest - Pistol Creek Ranch: Sam Hopkins journeyed to the Middle Fork country as a packer in 1892. He built the first cabin on the flat below Pistol Creek and ran a string of mules for the Lost Packer Mine in the region. Sam was mistaken for a bear and shot twice by a cross-eyed hunter. He survived, but never recovered enough continue the rough work of mining and packing.

   Eleck and Martha Watson, the grandparents of Fred Paulson and Daisy Tappan, bought the cabin from Sam. They sold it to the Risleys from New York who filed a homestead claim for 144 acres in 1920. The ranch passed through several more owners and ended up in the hands of Bill and Adelade Wayne. They built a two-story lodge on the property that burned down in 1955.

   Marvin Hornback and his wife Barbara leased and eventually bought the place from the Waynes. By 1964 they had cleared the airstrip, surveyed and subdivided the 144 acres, and made several additions to the property. They floated supplies downstream for a Pelton Wheel power generator and sawmill. They cut lumber on site for several cabins and sold quarter-acre riverfront lots for $18,000.

   Marvin was killed in a plane crash, and several of the lot owners formed a corporation to buy the remaining property from Barbara. When the Idaho Wilderness Act passed in 1980, the private land at the Pistol Creek Ranch was "grandfathered" into the Wilderness and the property remains in private ownership today.

   After the 2000 fires destroyed all but a few of the cabins, the Forest Service worked closely with the corporation to manage the rebuilding. New structures had to meet specific design requirements. Homeowners who chose to move back from the river's edge could add square footage to their original floorplan. As of 2005 about half of the original 17 cabins had been rebuilt.

Mile 22.2 - Pistol Creek Camp: (646517E 4953880N): Pull in to the sand/gravel bar on river left at the end of the Pistol Creek Gorge. This camp has great swimming and cliff jumping into the deep pools. The Little Pistol fires burned this camp completely in August of 2000, and the Forest Service closed it for several years. Over 30 "hazard trees" were cut down before re-opening the camp. Hike up Pistol Creek to witness Mother Nature's recovery first hand.

Mile 22.1 - Pistol Creek Rapid: Once you pass Lake Creek Rapid, Pistol Creek is two quick turns downstream. The river speeds into a tight s-turn veering hard left to avoid bedrock ledges before crashing into the left hand "Pistol Wall" (see diagram on page 57). Hike downstream from the Lake Creek debris fan or Huntington Dredge to the scout overlook. There are numerous vantages to photograph Pistol Creek Rapid. Run first and allow 10 to 15 minutes for setup on either side of the river.
High Water – (Class IV) Enter right at the top and aim for the big pillow piling off the "Bedrock Point" right of center. Forward push through the left side of the pillow and carry momentum past the "Pistol Wall". Essentially you push a straight line through the dollar sign s-turn. Alternatively, you can back pull as described for low water.
Low Water – (Class III+) Below 3.5 feet more bedrock ledges emerge creating a well defined S-turn. Pull away from the right hand ledges but watch out for the "Shark Rock" on the river left. Pivot quickly and pull off the left hand wall. 3.5 feet is a difficult stage for this rapid (especially in a Sweep Boat) as the s-turn is well defined with fast current. Use proper spacing.

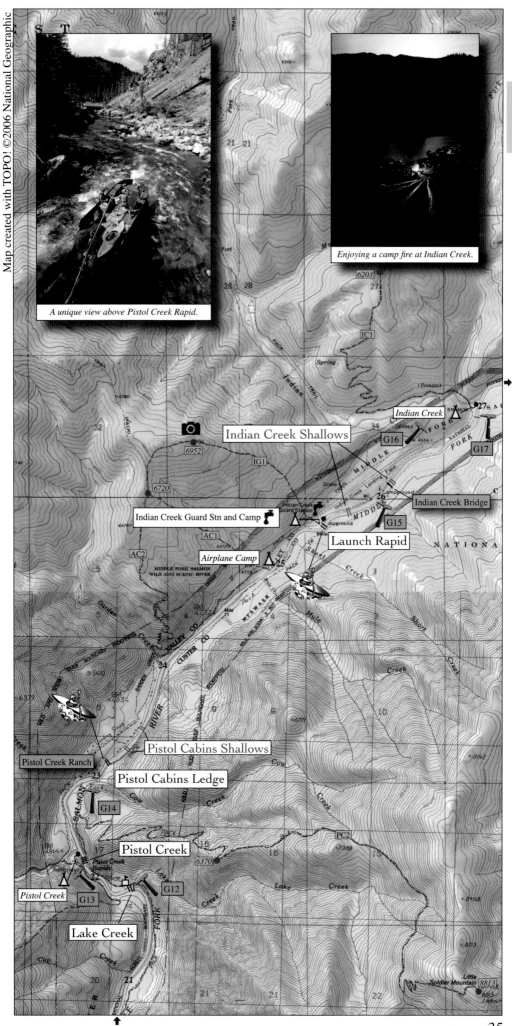

Map created with TOPO! ©2006 National Geographic

A unique view above Pistol Creek Rapid.

Enjoying a camp fire at Indian Creek.

Indian Creek Shallows

Indian Creek

G16

G17

Indian Creek Bridge

Indian Creek Guard Stn and Camp

G15

Launch Rapid

Airplane Camp

Pistol Cabins Shallows

Pistol Creek Ranch

Pistol Cabins Ledge

G14

Pistol Creek

PC2

G12

G13

Pistol Creek

Lake Creek

Mile 31.7 - Little Soldier Camp: (655993E 4955504N) Just downstream from the mouth of Little Soldier Creek is a gravel bar dominated by a huge ponderosa tree. There are two flat benches uphill for tent sites. The gravel bar is covered above 6 feet forcing you to carry the kitchen to the upper benches. This is a hot camp in August but the swimming hole provides instant relief from the sun.

Mile 31.6 - Little Soldier Rapid: (Class II-) A series of bedrock ledges forms a small rapid on a sharp right hand turn above Little Soldier Creek. There is some fun ledge-hole surfing at lower flows.

Mile 29.3 - Higby's Rock (Teapot Rapid): A short straightaway separates these two rapids.
At high water this is a fun Class II+.
Low Water - (Class II-) Run the middle slot moving from center towards the left bank. During the drought years of the early nineties, commercial trips launched from Thomas Creek at low water partially because this small rapid became nearly impassable.

Mile 29.1 - Oreland Rapid (Oreo): One mile below Pungo Rapid look for an eroded debris fan at the mouth of Orelano Creek on river right. I have seen the creek spew debris into the river several times in the past 15 years. The largest event occurred during an intense thunderstorm in 2002 when a debris flow poured tons of rocks, mud, and logs into the river to create a new rapid (see G19 on page 87).
High Water – (Class III-) This rapid marks the beginning of a long stretch of fun, continuous Class II and III water through the rest of Pungo Canyon. Read and run along the right side.
Low Water – (Class II+) The 2005 configuration of this evolving landslide rapid has a large pile of rubble in the middle.   Below 3 feet the right channel is clogged with angular rocks, and the left is split by a large blocky pour-over boulder. Below the entrance work right of center and run center over the bedrock falls downstream.
CAUTION - The blocky rock snags many IKs in the entrance, so be ready for a mid-rapid rescue.

Mile 28.2 - Pungo Rapid: (Class II-) This medium to low water rapid forms on the left bank at the end of the Pungo Pool. The river drains left, pinches against the bank and forms a small wave train. In the early nineties, a large submerged rock called the "Pungo Maiden" started to appear. Avoiding this sharp, boat-tearing rock at low water was always a challenge. Rafters built small rock levees to deepen the approach during the drought years from '91 to '94
   Over time the gravel bar shifted and the Pungo Maiden formed a flat, but powerful keeper hole. I watched an eighteen foot cargo boat flat spin for two minutes in the Maiden's clutches!
   As of this writing, Pungo is a fun wave train with quirky hydraulics along the left bank. At low water watch out for the sharp tip of the Maiden because she is still there, waiting for the upstream gravels to shift again in her favor.

Mile 28.2 - Point of Interest - Pungo Mine: Cross Pungo Creek and follow a trail up the bench to a stone foundation. From here a steep trail leads to a unique, hard-rock, mine shaft that follows a vein of fluorspar over a hundred feet into the hillside. Several tailing piles can be found on the bench below.
   In 1933 John Minshew took over a quartz claim on the hillside here. A trapper by profession, John built two cabins and tended a large garden. He made nearly $500 a season by selling martin pelts.
   In 1936 Eddie Budell joined John in his trapping operation. In the off-season, they both worked for the Lucky Lad Mine in the Forty-Five Creek drainage. Both men left the Middle Fork to enlist in the military during WWII. John found a railroad job in Pocatello and decided not to return to the Middle Fork. Ed failed his draft examinations and returned to the cabins on Pungo Creek.
   Ed worked a pack string and built trail for the Forest Service between 1943 and 1950. In the winters he poked into the hillside above the cabin, exploring the mineral wealth of his claim. A spectrographic analysis from Boise identified the mineral to be a high-grade fluorspar which is used to make hydrofluoric acid. Metallic-grade fluorspar is used in steel production. It is a scarce mineral in the US, so Ed became excited about the value of his claim.
   He drove three shafts into the hillside. The longest was over 100 feet, but the vein eventually pinched out. He prospected for a continuation of the vein across the river in hopes of generating enough interest in the mine to justify building a road to the claim. He never found it.
   Without a road, Ed looked into the prospect of packing the ore to the Indian Creek Airstrip and flying 3000 pounds at a time out of the Middle Fork. After crunching the numbers, Ed realized he could only break even, so he halted this plan after building several wooden docks to load the mules.
   In the early fifties, Ed sold his claim to the Fluorspar Corporation in Reno, Nevada. They held an option on developing the mine, but plans never came to fruition. The mining claims were allowed to lapse, so no further development will take place. Ed eventually retired to Lake Lowell, ID. The cabins were burned by the Forest Service.

Mile 28.2 - Pungo Camp: (652478E 4958603N) Pull in just below the mouth of Pungo creek to access this nice camp among the trees. It is a culturally sensitive area so please follow F.S. camping regulations.

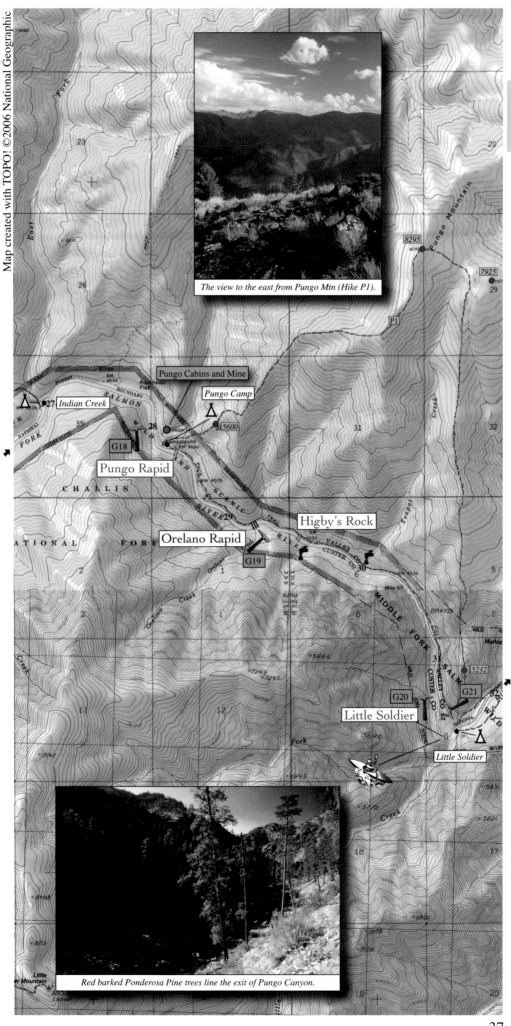

Map created with TOPO! ©2006 National Geographic

The view to the east from Pungo Mtn (Hike P1).

Pungo Cabins and Mine

Pungo Camp

Indian Creek

G18

Pungo Rapid

Higby's Rock

Orelano Rapid

G19

Little Soldier

G20

G21

Little Soldier

Red barked Ponderosa Pine trees line the exit of Pungo Canyon.

37

Mile 37.5 - Jackass Shallows: Stay along the right bank in this wide flat.

Mile 36.6 - Hood Ranch Camp: (658829E 4954802N) Pull in on the left bank just below the island. This camp and the hot springs were altered by the Sunflower Creek debris flow in 2002. There is an old homestead cabin on the upstream end of the bench.

Mile 36.5 - Point of Interest – Hood Ranch Cabin: See next page

Mile 36.4 - Little Creek Camp: (658492E 4954653N). This camp sits up on a bench above the river. Pull-in to the right bank below the Guard Station and bridge. There are several old downed trees along the bank that will dictate where you can land. You can visit the Guard Station and Little Creek Cabins from here.

Mile 36.2 Point of Interest – Little Creek Cabins: See next page.

Mile 36 - Little Creek Guard Station: Fred Paulson was originally hired by the Forest Service to pack in the supplies for the bridge. A deep spring snowpack prevented an early start so they hired Bob Johnson to fly in the materials instead.

Mile 35.6 - Stateland Right Camp: (658160E 4953846N) Get ready for a swift pull-in on an inside right corner. The camp sits among a sprawling Ponderosa grove. Several large trees blew down during a windstorm in 2002. I had a friend in camp that afternoon who started running in the wrong direction. He made it to the river's edge before the upper branches of the falling tree knocked him down in the shallow water. Miraculously, he was unhurt.

Mile 35.4 - Stateland Left Camp: (658008 4953652N) This low, Ponderosa Pine-covered bench sprawls along the bank for over 1000 yards. At high flows look for a swift landing at a steep gravel bar on the downstream end of the bench. At low water pull in further upstream below a large boulder in the river and carry across the long gravel bar to camp.

Mile 35 - Thomas Creek Shallows: After it passes the mouth of Thomas Creek, the river will bend to the left. Cut left across the top of the gravel bar to avoid dragging your boats.

Mile 35 - Point of Interest - Middle Fork Lodge & Bridge: Tom and Nell McCall, one time owners of the property, rebuilt the bridge sometime in the early 40's The Middle Fork gauge reading is taken from the bridge. See the next page for more history.

Mile 33.7 - Sunflower Shallows: Starting around 3, feet run on river left after passing the hot springs.

Mile 33.6 - Lost Oak Camp: (656931E 4954968N) Perched on a high bench across from Sunflower Flat Hot Springs, this camp has a long carry. The upshot is the proximity to the hot spring shower across the river. Pull in on the left bank around the corner at the end of the pool.

Mile 33.6 - Sunflower Flat Camp: (656867E 4954944N) A few tent sites are carved out of the rocky terrain for a small group at this hot springs camp. Pull in to the deep eddy downstream of the shower. It used to be known as "Pottie's Spring" for Sylvester Potvein who had a cabin nearby. Share respectfully with other groups camped here.

Mile 33 - Ski Jump Rapid: This is a narrow constriction rapid beneath a towering cliff on river right a half mile below Marble Creek.
Extreme Water – (Class IV) Ski Jump is one of the largest and most powerful rapids on the river above 8-9 feet. The sloping cliff on river left creates a boat flipping reflex wave that merges with a monstrous hole formed by "Ski Jump Rock" in the center of the river. Run between furious eddy fences down the right side.
Low Water - (Class II) The right hand channel clogs with boulders around 3 feet. Experienced rafters can play with the boil that piles onto the downsloping face of Ski Jump rock in the center.

Mile 32.7 - Marble Right Camp: (656969E 4956294N) Pull in to a powerful but small eddy on the inside right below the mouth of Marble Creek. The sand and gravel bar has limited tent sites, but there are two benches above with plenty of room.

Mile 32.5 - Marble Creek Rapid (Chipmunk): (Class III-) The placid pool and narrow choke between good cliff jumps signals that Marble Creek rapid is downstream. Run left of center at all levels. There is excellent kayak surfing in this rapid. Scout from Marble Left camp. *CAUTION:* The right side of a bedrock ledge forms a nasty keeper hole around 3.5 feet. Below 2.5 feet the upper two holes frequently tip IKs.
   The name "Chipmunk" originated when Oregon guide Jack Lowry was caught in the ledge hole. It was rumored that he looked like a chipmunk scurrying along the handrail of his driftboat to keep it from flipping. This is an easy rapid to photograph from the river left ledge.

Mile 32.4 - Marble Left Camp: (656642E 4956406N) At lower flows use the pull-in below the small cliff band on river left to access the large grassy bench. It is fun to watch passing groups run Marble Creek Rapid from your riverside kitchen. In 2005 there was a fallen tree along the bank that complicated this pull-in.

Mile 32.3 - Upper Marble Left Camp: (656511E 4956234N) There is a pull-in on the top left of the Marble Pool that should be used during high water to access the upper end of the Marble Creek bench. The broad bench 30 feet above the river has ample room for tents.

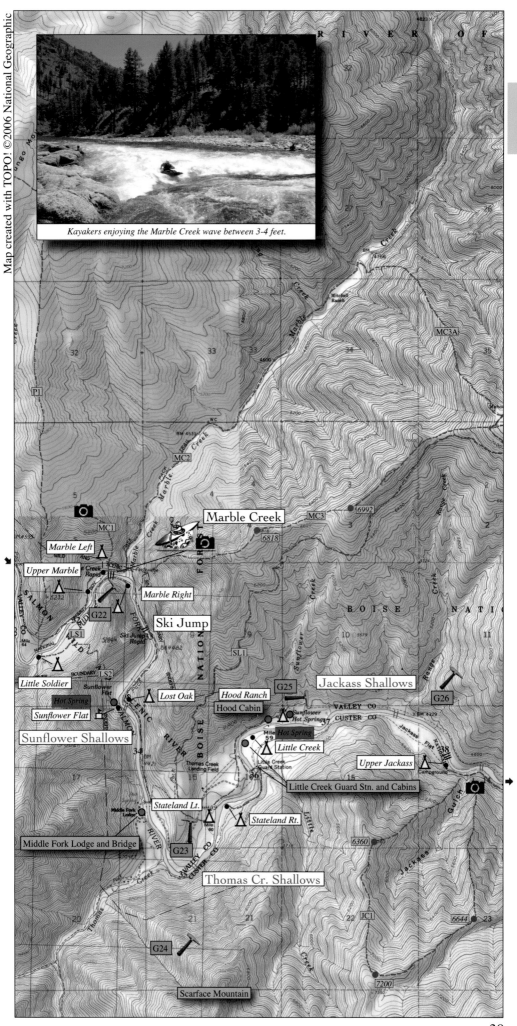

Map created with TOPO! ©2006 National Geographic

Kayakers enjoying the Marble Creek wave between 3-4 feet.

MC3A

P1

MC2

MC1

Marble Creek

MC3

6992

6818

Marble Left

Upper Marble

Marble Right

G22

Ski Jump

LS1

SL1

LS2

Little Soldier

Lost Oak

Hood Ranch
Hood Cabin

G25

Jackass Shallows

G26

Hot Spring

Sunflower Flat

Sunflower Shallows

Sunflower Hot Spring

VALLEY CO
CUSTER CO

Hot Spring

Little Creek

Upper Jackass

Little Creek Guard Stn. and Cabins

Stateland Lt.

Middle Fork Lodge and Bridge

G23

Stateland Rt.

6360

Thomas Cr. Shallows

JC1

6644

G24

7200

Scarface Mountain

Thomas Creek Area History

Hood Ranch Cabins: John Chestnut first settled this bar. He built a cabin, planted peach trees, and sold the fruit to miners in the region. Milt and Mary Hood moved down from the Middle Fork Lodge and built a new outfitting cabin with hot running water piped across from Sunflower Hot spring. They left in 1942. The property now belongs to the State Fish and Game Department.

Little Creek Cabins: The cabins downstream of the Little Creek Guard Station were built by Jim and Belle Hash. They ran a string of pack animals selling produce from Custer to the Thunder Mountain mine. The cabins are presently owned by the Middle Fork Lodge.

Middle Fork Lodge & Bridge: The open landscape and numerous flat terraces in the vicinity of Thomas Creek made for a storied history. The creek itself was named by miners in the 1880's. In 1900 Jim Bollard from England and Mac McNerney of Ireland first developed the land. They mined the creek and built a two story cabin and barn on the flat above the river. They had several horses and 50 head of cattle that grazed on the ample, grassy flats in the area. The mining claims, buildings, hayfields, and livestock were sold in 1913.

The buyers, Freeman Nethkin and Edward Osborne worked the area as a cattle ranch before selling their interest to the Middle Fork Land and Livestock Company in 1919.

With connections to the Overland National Bank in Boise, ID, The MFL & L Co. hoped to make Thomas Creek the headquarters for a large livestock operation. They bought the grazing rights from all the ranches as far downstream as Loon Creek, and brought in 1200 sheep to winter on the canyon grasses.

Starting in late October the company led 300 cattle out of the canyon via the Pistol Creek Trail over the pass to Cascade. They ran into one of the most severe winters on record. The trip lasted until December, and most of the cattle died en route. Of the 1200 sheep wintering in the Middle Fork, only 300 survived.

MFL & L Co. went bankrupt, and the property changed hands several times. Milt Hood built the airstrip in 1934-35 to support the first Middle Fork hunting and fishing lodge. Tom and Nell McCall later developed a sawmill and power generator. A new lodge was built in 1943.

The Lodge ended up in the hands of Bill Harrah of Harrah's Casinos, who used it to entertain friends and employees until 1978. He ran a riverside concession for many years, selling ice cream and soda pop to rafters floating by. The Nature Conservancy worked with the existing owners to limit the development potential through easements. The riverside store was closed.

It has changed hands twice since then. The current owner has improved several of the cabins, upgraded the facilities and runs the operation as a wilderness hunting and fishing lodge.

Mile 42.2 - Mahoney Camp: (664907E 4957378N) The river bends left after the long (low water) boulder garden that parallels the Mahoney airstrip. Look for a small beach on the inside right of the next turn. The water boils into a small bedrock cliff on the opposite bank.

Mile 41.3 - Point of Interest – Cougar Creek Ranch: Thought to have been built by Dutch John Helmke, this site was purchased in 1924 by Charley and Wilma Warnock. They ran cattle on the grassy flat here and downstream at the Mahoney Ranch, which they also owned. They sold the property to the Fish and Game Department.

Mile 40.1 - Point of Interest - Cameron Creek Camp and Pictographs: (663041E 4955195N) Directly across from Little Loon Creek, this small camp on a rocky bank is a popular cultural stop. There are pictographs at the base of a cliff above camp, and several pit-house depressions on the flat just downstream. The pull-in below a class I+ riffle catches some people off guard.

Mile 38.7 - Lower Jackass Camp: (661401E 4954138N) This long, shady shoreline on the right bank below Jackass Island is a culturally sensitive site, so camping is not permitted on the high bench. At very high flows most of this camp will be under water. At low water there is a large gravel bar upstream, or a pull-in 200 yards below to an open, rocky, shoreline.

Mile 38.5 - Jackass Island Rapid: (Class II-) There is a wide gravel island on a right turn below Jackass Rapid. Run right at low water.

Mile 38.1 - Upper Jackass Camp: (660735E 4954339N). Pull in just below Jackass Rapid on the right bank. This sand bar and low bench has several great tent sites tucked among the trees.

Mile 38 - Jackass Rapid:
A log jam piled atop a bedrock shelf on river left is your identifier for the rapid just downstream.

High Water – (Class III) Jackass is formed by jagged bedrock ledges that protrude from the left bank. There is a large boulder downstream of the main rapid in the center of the river. At high water the ledges are covered by a large wave train. *CAUTION* - Between 5 and 6 feet, the downstream boulder forms a large hole in the middle of the wave train. Watch out!

Low Water – (Class III-) Below 3 feet the ledges emerge, and a right bank gravel bar forces an entry left of center. Hug inside along the gravel bar and pull hard right before the ledges.

CAUTION - Pay special attention to the IKs as they tend to drift left and get hung up on the bedrock ledges. It is difficult for Sweep Boats to make this low water cut.

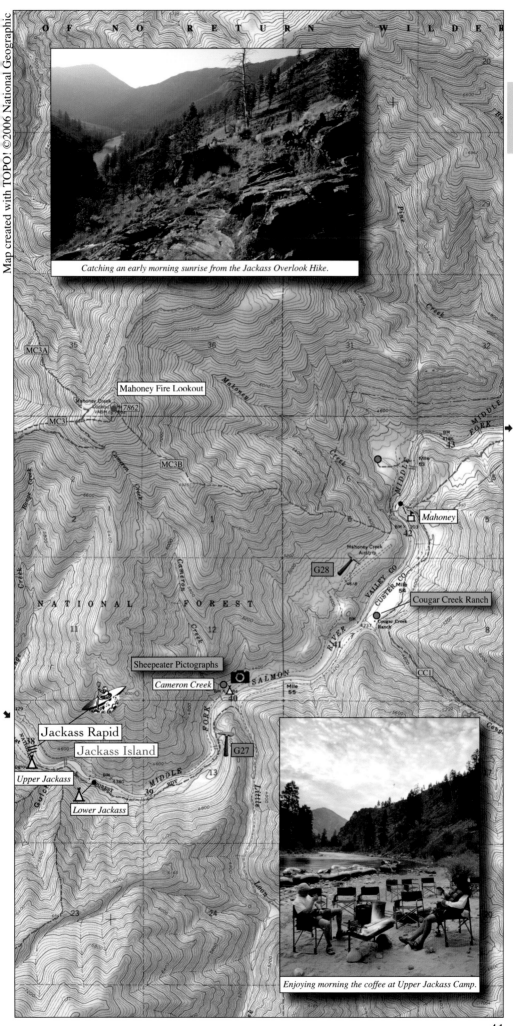

O F   N O   R E T U R N   W I L D E R

Catching an early morning sunrise from the Jackass Overlook Hike.

MC3A

Mahoney Fire Lookout

MC3

MC3B

N A T I O N A L   F O R E S T

G28

Mahoney

Cougar Creek Ranch

CC1

Sheepeater Pictographs

Cameron Creek

SALMON

Jackass Rapid

Jackass Island

G27

Upper Jackass

MIDDLE FORK

Lower Jackass

Enjoying morning the coffee at Upper Jackass Camp.

41

Mile 47 - Rock Island Camp: (669818E 4961032N): This timbered bench is on the inside-left bank below the White E. Cox Pool. Run the inside channel at high water, and get ready for a fast pull-in. This is a Native American cultural site. Please respect the camping restrictions.

Mile 46.9 - Gravel Island and Rock Island Rock: (Class II+) This location has seen significant changes in the past 15 years. High water in '96 and '97 opened the channel along the left bank. In 2001 and 2002 the current ran directly into the rock at the bottom, wrapping at least one boat on the front of "Rock Island Rock." The current has since shifted to the right. Treat this left channel with caution. IK's should use the safer right hand channel.

Mile 46.8 - Whitie Cox Camp: (669573E 4961074N). This sand and gravel beach on the inside-right bank is dominated by a huge, shady Ponderosa tree. The beach is mostly covered at high water, but spacious at low flows. The pool is a fantastic swimming hole in mid-summer. The higher bench has numerous river-view tent sites. Watch out for the poison ivy along the trail to the hot spring which has been plagued by strawberry mites in the past. A quick dip in the river will scare them off.

Mile 46.8 - Point of Interest - Whitie Cox Gravestone: Elvis "Whitie" Cox worked as a packer for the Costal Geodetic Survey until the start of WWII. After serving as an infantryman, he tried to ease back into civilian life. He worked at a bakery in Twin Falls before heading back to the Middle Fork to appease his introverted personality. Whitie had diverted water from the hot springs to work a placer mine along the river when the bank collapsed and buried him alive. He was buried on the bench above.

Mile 46.6 - Whitie Cox Shallows: Pick an impossible line through the rocks along the left bank below 2 feet.

Mile 46.2 - Screaming Right Hand Turn (SRT) #2 (Culver Creek Rapid): (Class II) After it passes a beautiful shaded waterfall on the right bank, the river appears choked with a string of large boulders. Follow the same route as in SRT#1, and trust that a channel on the far left bank will materialize.

Mile 46 - Culver Creek Camp: (668796E 4960679N) This is a small, sandy bench nestled among several large Ponderosa trees. This camp is nearly impossible to access at low water due to the shallow landing.

Mile 45 - Red Bluff Shallows: Just downstream of the Red Bluff rocks is a low water trap. Stay left and float on deep water among several huge boulders.

Mile 44.9 - Red Bluff Rocks: A reddish pink cliff towers 200 feet above the river on the right bank. Several beautifully polished black rocks clog the river and form holes at high water.

Mile 44 - Lower Pine Flat Rapid: This small rapid at the end of the pool below Pine Flat Camp is an easy riffle at higher flows.
Low Water - (Class II+) At flows below 2 feet this riffle is riddled with tricky shelf rock. The stylish "Zorro Run" enters left over a pour-over ledge. The cleanest channel then cuts all the way to the right bank before pulling hard back to center at the very bottom of the run.

Mile 43.8 - Point of Interest - Fred Paulson's Cabin: Follow the trail downstream and uphill to Fred Paulson's cabin. It is tucked in among the trees at the mouth of a small canyon.
   Fred spent many years as a child living with his grandparents at Indian Creek. The family relocated to Green River, UT where Fred and his sister Daisy went to school. Fred returned to the Middle Fork in the thirties and spent much of his life living and packing up and down the canyon. He was renowned for his kind demeanor and tremendous strength (notice the size of his cabin logs!)

Mile 43.8 - Pine Flat Camp: (666565E 4958540N) This high bench has a narrow, but easy pull-in on the right bank downstream of the Pine Flat Pool. It's an awkward carry up a sloping granite ledge to a spacious grass and rocky bench. The swimming pool offers relief from the hot August sun.

Mile 43.7 - Pine Flat Pool Exit: (Class II-) The low water challenge is to make a clean run through the boulders on river left. There is an easy center or right hand channel.

Mile 43.6 - Pine Flat Rapid: (Class II+) About .5 miles below SRT #1 the river rushes past a small reddish cliff on the right bank forming a wave train that pushes left toward the bank. Starting at 4.5 feet, watch out for a large bedrock boulder at the end of the wave train. Pull or push into the boiling eddy inside right for a high speed eddy turn. This is a great ender spot for kayaks at nearly all levels, and fun for paddleboats below 3 feet. It is easy to set up for some kayak close-up photos at this spot.

Mile 43.3 - Screaming Right-Hand Turn (SRT) #1: (Class II) As the water drops below 4 feet, the river appears clogged with boulders. Drift left with the current, and you will find a channel along the left bank. I have seen boats wrapped on the larger boulders as a result of last minute indecision. Pay attention to novice IKs here on this easy water day.

Mile 42.5 - Point of Interest – Mahoney Ranch: Pull over in the eddy below the small rapid downstream of Mahoney Camp. Prior to the 1924 purchase by the Warnock's (Cougar Creek Ranch), Ray Mahoney lived on this bench. He planted a small fruit orchard above the river. It is a nice walk up the bench to wander around and look for remnants of Mahoney's early homestead.

Rock Island Rock

Whitie Cox Shallows

SRT #2

Red Bluff Shallows

Red Bluff Rocks

G30

Lower Pine Flat

G29

Mahoney Ranch

Fred Paulson's Cabin

SRT #1

Pine Flat

Pine Flat Pool Exit

Pine Flat Rapid

Mahoney

Culver Creek

Rock Island

Whitie Cox Grave-
stone and Camp

Whitie's Grave Marker

Beautiful mammatus clouds threaten rain.

43

Mile 52.8 - Hospital Bar Surf Hole: (Class II+) This feature on the right bank below the hot springs forms between 2 and 3 feet. It has an awkward diagonal horizon line that flips many IKs. Hardshell kayaks will have a great surf session here. The hole can be avoided to the left.

Mile 52.6 - Cave Camp: (674516E 4967091N) Located on the inside bend of the 180-degree turn above Hospital Bar, this small sand and gravel camp has three or four good tent sites at low water. You will have to share the hot springs with the Hospital Bar campers.

Mile 51.1 - Underwater Canyon: (Class II) The second bend below Cow Camp has a low water rapid. Run left of center to avoid grounding on bedrock ledges. Float over the top of a beautiful 20 foot deep underwater canyon downstream. Swimming with a mask through the canyon is a thrilling ride. A small trail leads to some pictographs on the left wall above the rapid. Climb to the top of the cliff with your camera and a polarized lens for a beautiful photo opportunity.

Mile 50.8 - Cow Camp Riffle: (Class II) Read and run.

Mile 50.7 - Cow Camp: (673361E 4964685N) Look for a rocky pull-in on the right bank just upstream of several reddish cliff outcrops. Please follow Forest Service camping regulations for this culturally sensitive site.

Mile 50.1 - Big Loon Camp: (673044E 4963965N) The large gravel bar at the mouth of Loon Creek has tent sites tucked among the hawthorn bushes and on a grassy bench uphill by the fence. Prepare for a hard pull across the Loon Creek current at high water. The hot springs up Loon Creek are not to be missed. Photogenic sunsets can be spectacular from this camp.

Gold was discovered in1869 on Loon creek by three men from Leesburg, Idaho. It sparked a migration to the drainage typical of the west coast gold fever that began in the tailrace of Sutters Mill near Sacramento, CA. Just 4 years later, in 1873, there were 600 claims on Loon creek and the town of Oro Grande grew to 15,000 inhabitants.

In February of 1879 five Chinese miners were killed in this rough-and-tumble mining environment. Their deaths, blamed on the native Sheepeater Indians, sparked a multi-year military campaign to apprehend the murderers and "bring them to justice." Due to both the mining and military activity, Loon Creek Canyon became one of the main arteries of traffic to and from the Middle Fork Canyon.

Bob Ramey lived at the confluence of Loon Creek with the Middle Fork. With plentiful sunshine and readily available water, Ramey made the most of this opportune location on the river. He diverted water from Cache Creek for his garden and hay fields that supported nearly 100 head of cattle.

Like most along the Middle Fork, the place has changed hands several times over the years. Sam and Amie Lovell raised horses on the bench and sold them to the military at Fort Boise. The Lovells sold to Bob Simplot who transferred it to his brother Jack. Jack kept the cabins but sold the rest to the Fish and Game.

Mile 49 – Jack Creek Rapid: (Class II) This small lake and rapid downstream were formed as a result of rain induced landslides in 2002. Run right (See page 84 and G33 on page 89 for more detail).

Mile 49.2 - Loon Islands: (Class II) This wide gravel deposit is split by three channels. The entire island will be covered at 7 to 8 feet. The right hand channel shuts off around 4 feet, the middle channel below 3 feet, leaving only the left channel at lower flows.

Mile 48.9 - Shelf Camp: (671286E 4963179N). Pull in to a gravel bar landing to access the upstream end of a large tree-covered bench. At low flows there is a spacious kitchen beneath the giant Ponderosa tree.

Mile 48.7 - Shelf Rapid: This small, bedrock rapid forms at the end of the pool beneath the White Creek Bridge. A beautiful glassy surf wave for kayaks forms around 3.5 feet.

Mile 48.8 - White Creek Bridge: Both sides of the river are flanked by flat, 50-foot river terraces. In the early nineties an experienced backcountry pilot had an engine fail while flying in the canyon. Fortunately, he managed to set his plane down on the limited flat ground along the left bank and walked away unharmed.

Mile 48.1 - White Creek Camp: (670715E 4962185N) Pull in just below the island at the bottom of White Creek Rapid. This is a culturally sensitive site, so please camp on the lower bench among Ponderosa trees. There are more tent sites in the sandy riparian alcoves downstream (covered at high water). Explore the American Indian pit-house depressions on the higher, upstream bench.

Mile 48 - White Creek Rapid: Look for a 90-degree left-hand turn with a small water-worn cliff outcrop on the inside bank. The rapid starts below.
High Water - (Class II) Stay left of center at high water. There is often a log jam clogging the right side of small island at the bottom.
Low Water - (Class II+) Tricky below 2 feet!! Leave the upper pool following a center channel over a deep underwater chasm in the bedrock. Just before it ends, cut left and carry speed along the bank over several rocks. Don't get suckered into the dead-end channels leading back to center.

Mile 47.1 - Rock Island Shallows: Just below Rock Island Camp, push across the top of the gravel shallows to get to deeper water along the left bank.

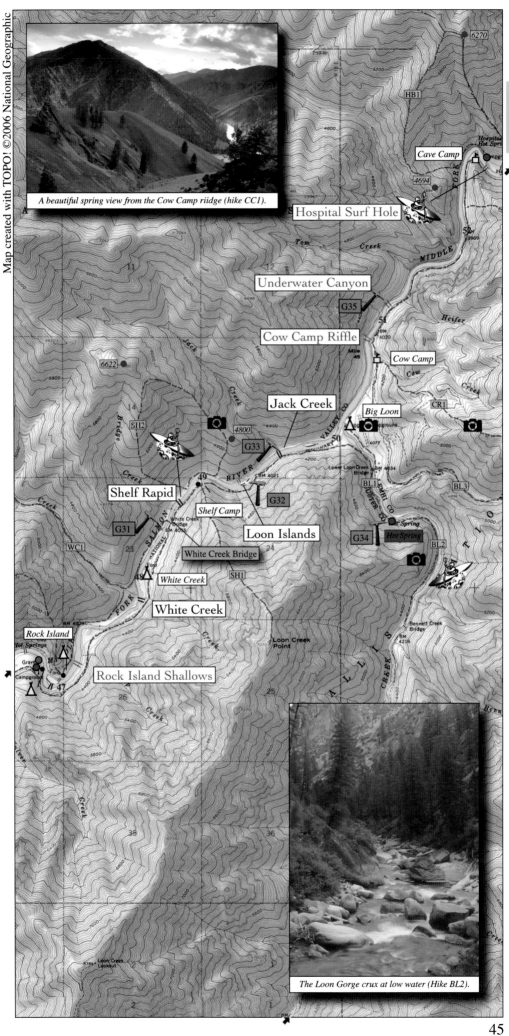

A beautiful spring view from the Cow Camp riidge (hike CC1).

Cave Camp

Hospital Surf Hole

HB1

6270

4694

Underwater Canyon

G35

Cow Camp Riffle

Cow Camp

Heifer

CR1

Big Loon

Jack Creek

G33

4800

Shelf Rapid

SH12

G32

Loon Islands

Shelf Camp

BL1

BL3

Hot Spring

G34

BL2

G31

White Creek Bridge

WC1

White Creek

SH1

White Creek

Rock Island

Rock Island Shallows

The Loon Gorge crux at low water (Hike BL2).

Mile 60.5 - Camas Creek Shallows: Enter along the left bank across from the Camas Creek Camp, and look for a hidden channel that works towards the center 25 to 30 feet right of a large dry boulder. When leaving Camas Creek Camp DON'T drift downstream. Walk or row your boats to the left channel to set up for the run. Use proper spacing.

Mile 60.3 - Camas Creek Camp (Ant Row): (679829E 4973426N) Camas Creek is a hot spot in mid-summer. It offers a large shade Ponderosa and great swimming in the creek upstream. The trail down Camas Creek served as another major artery into the Middle Fork from Meyers Cove more than twenty miles up the canyon.

Mile 59.3 - Tappan IV: (Class II) Turn the left corner below Tappan III, and run a small rapid with a huge pointed boulder left of center. Drift, swim, and celebrate in the pool below this final rapid. There is a great canyon photo opportunity from the pool below.

Mile 59 - Tappan III: (Class III-) See the next page for a diagram and description.

Mile 58.9 - Tappan II (Fish and Game Rock): See the next page for a diagram and description.

Mile 58.5 - Tappan Falls: See the next page for a diagram and description. There are great opportunities for photography from the scout along the right bank.

Mile 58.2 - Tappan I Rapid: The 90-degree right turn below the Tappan Canyon Entrance Rapid marks the beginning of the Tappan series. The grey cliff on the inside corner displays some beautiful striped metamorphic rock.
High Water - (Class III-) Run center and work left of center at the bottom to avoid crashing into the cliff wall at bottom right.
Low Water - (Class II+) Watch out for the bottom center hole around 3 feet. Below 2 feet enter right of center before cutting to the right bank along the cliff wall. Ship your right oar and hug the bank before working back to the middle for the finish.

Mile 58 - Tappan Canyon Entrance Rapid: (Class II+) A half mile below Tappan Island the river makes a sharp left turn beneath an 800 foot grey cliff wall. Just upstream and right of center is a large wave train and ledge hole. Stay left of these features to set up for the sharp turn. Pull inside to avoid large metamorphic boulders right of center downstream. There is good kayak surfing potential in the ledge hole.

Mile 57.5 - Tappan Island Camp: (676889E 4971470N) A unique camp, Tappan Island is spacious and rarely used. Pull in at the top of the island, or along the right bank at lower flows.

Mile 57.1 - Point of Interest – Fred and Daisy Paulson-Tappan's Homestead: Having grown up along the Middle Fork, Daisy returned to the river just like her brother Fred Paulson. She and her husband Fred Tappan bought the ranch from Willis Bill Jones sometime in the thirties for $1200. Jones had established a fruit orchard that was already bearing fruit.
   Daisy and Fred expanded the ranch by diverting water from Grouse Creek to additional fruit trees, a large garden, and two hayfields behind the cabin. They had several head of cattle as well. The Tappans were almost entirely self sufficient. Fred worked at the Yellowjacket Mine so they could afford to buy horseshoes, leather, and clothes.
   When their boys were old enough to start school, the Tappans moved closer to civilization. Daisy ran a dog sled for a mine near the town of Yellow Pine. She eventually settled in the Pahsimeroi Valley. Their ranch on the Middle Fork was arguably the most successful and reliably run homestead on the river.

Mile 57.1 - Lower Grouse Camp: (676344E 4971194N) This large sand bar is tucked against a row of beautiful trees. The old-growth Ponderosa Pine centerpiece blew down in 2004 and still lays across a good portion of the beach. Pull in right to an eddy in the middle of Grouse Creek rapid. It is a fast landing, so give each boat plenty of room before entering the rapid. The eddy gets smaller as the river drops.

Mile 57 - Grouse Creek Rapid: (Class II+) The pool at the end of the Grouse Necks drains into this s-turn rapid with fast-moving choppy water at higher flows. At 3 feet the rapid becomes a fast-moving boulder garden. Hug inside right to make the pull-in for Lower Grouse Creek camp. There is a good kayak surf wave at the bottom of the rapid starting at 3 feet. Use proper spacing.

Mile 56.8 - Upper Grouse Camp: (676283E 4971056N) This sand and gravel beach has several tent sites on the grassy bench it shares with Lower Grouse Camp. There is little shade here.

Mile 54 - Cub Creek Waves: Below Cub Creek is a narrow constriction between a vertical cliff wall on the right and enormous 30 foot high boulders on the left. There is a small lunch beach at low water on the right bank just past the cliff wall.
Extreme Water - (Class IV-) At flows above 8 feet I have heard reports of towering 20 foot waves below this river constriction.

Mile 53.7 - Cub Creek Camp: (675637E 4967443N) A rarely used camp sits on a low bench just above the high water line. Pull in on the left bank well above the mouth of Cub Creek.

Mile 53.3 - Horsetail Camp: (675086E 4967443N) This camp sits on a timbered bench above the river and just below the mouth of Big Aparajo Creek.

Mile 52.9 - Hospital Bar Camp: (674759E 4966907N) Pull in up or downstream to a spacious bench on the left bank below the hot springs. Bring a large tarp to augment the springs at lower flows, and be prepared for a windy afternoon. I've seen trees blow down, tents fly away, and an un-tethered paddle boat blow across the river here.

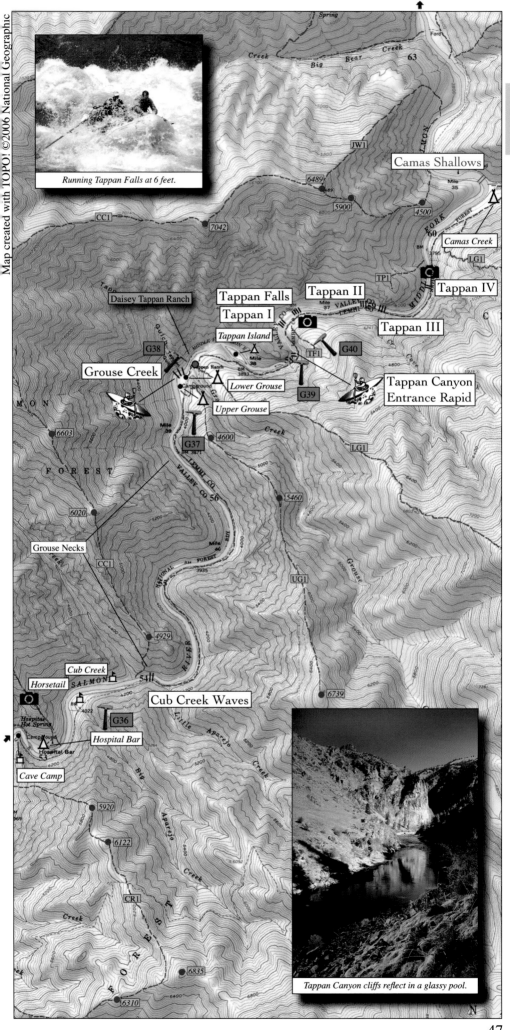

Running Tappan Falls at 6 feet.

Camas Shallows

JW1

CC1 — 7042

6489
6469
5900
4500
60 BM 3795

Camas Creek
LG1

TP1

Daisey Tappan Ranch

Tappan Falls
Tappan I
Tappan II
Tappan III
Tappan IV

Tappan Island

G38

Grouse Creek

Tappan Ranch
Mile 38
BM 3893

TF1
G40
G39

Lower Grouse

Upper Grouse

Tappan Canyon
Entrance Rapid

Mile 39
6603
G37
BM 3871
4600

6020

LG1

Grouse Necks
CC1

5460

Mile 36
BM
FOREST
3935

UG1

4929

RIVER

Cub Creek
Horsetail
SALMON
54

Cub Creek Waves

6739

Hospital
Hot Spring
G36

Hospital Bar

Hospital Bar
53

Cave Camp

5920

6122

CR1

6835

6310

F O R E S T

MON

FOREST

Tappan Canyon cliffs reflect in a glassy pool.

Mile 70.5 - Earthquake Rock: This rapid was created during the 1983 Borah Peak Earthquake, a magnitude 7 that shook Eastern Idaho. A large rock broke loose from the cliff band high on the right wall and splashed into the river. The rapid sits about halfway into the big left turn through Jack Creek Canyon.

High Water - (Class III-) At flows above 7 feet "Earthquake Rock" itself will form a significant hole right of center at the bottom. Work with the flow to the right of the rock/hole, or make a more committing forward push across the current to the left of the rock. A right line sneaks through the boulder garden along the right bank until 3 feet.

Low Water – (Class II+) The boulder garden forces entry further left, and a wave train forms in the current pushing towards E. Rock. Run inside right of the wave train, or push across the current to the left. Earthquake Rock becomes a wrap hazard as the water drops. There is a large pillow on the upstream side of the rock so if you miss your line, pivot to hit it straight on.

CAUTION - At low flows the innocuous "Boulder Seive" on the left bank presents a very dangerous strainer to kayaks. The left side of the uppermost wave tuns into a kayak tipping hole as the water drops. Swimmers here usually flush right, but I have seen a kayak, paddle, and swimmer strain left through these rocks. I have unclogged the same sieve of driftwood after the Bernard Creek blow out. Be aware.

Mile 59 - Tappan III: (Class III-) From the deep pool below "F&G Rock" look for a huge "Entrance Boulder" that splits the river into two channels. Twenty feet below, two more boulders ("Split Left" and "Split Right") divide the river again creating 4 possible routes: right-to-right, right-to-center, left-to-center, and left-to-left. Experienced rafters can run all possible lines at moderate flows. My personal favorite is left to center. The conservative line AT ALL FLOWS takes the left channel.

Low Water - (Class III) This becomes a tricky rapid at flows below 2 feet. Enter the channel left of the "Entrance Boulder" and push hard through several submerged rocks to the left bank.   Expect to get out and push over the "Rocky Shoals" below. For small boats the tight right-to-center line is a more committing but cleaner option at low water. The current pushes into "Split Left" harder than you think.

Mile 58.9 - Tappan II (Fish and Game Rock): The long straightaway below Tappan Falls ends in a constriction around the huge flat-faced "Fish and Game Rock." Just downstream a fence of boulders called "Buzzards Reef" extends from the left bank. There is a small "Kayak Slot" that splits the reef.

High Water - (Class III-) Run right of the large pillow/hole formed by "Fish and Game Rock." and just right of some large holes at "Buzzards Reef." Ride the boils off the cliff wall at the bottom. This run shuts off around 3.5 feet.

Low Water - (Class III) Run left of "F&G Rock" and pull hard to the right immediately downstream to avoid wrapping on "Buzzards Reef." I have seen boats stuff through the "Kayak Slot," but this is not the preferred run.   At flows below 2 feet the shallow gravel bar upstream pushes water into the left side of F&G Rock, so compensate for this current. Use proper spacing.

CAUTION - The "Kayak Slot" is an easy run for IKs, but is a significant hazard if plugged with a raft. Allow plenty of spacing in this rapid for both rafts and IKs.

Mile 58.5 - Tappan Falls: The pool below Tappan I ends at Tappan Falls, a large bedrock ledge that spans the entire river. Scout from river right. Run the right side at all flows.

High Water - (Class III+) Above 6 feet the falls are buried by a fun wave train. Watch out for large holes on river left. Until 3 feet place your right tube on the end of the "Small Whitecaps" deflecting off the bedrock upstream of the falls (right bank). Keep it straight down the v-tongue and work left past the drop.

Low Water – (Class IV-) At really low water, I have gotten stuck mid-falls, so scout your line carefully. A steep "Center Falls" is runnable left of the main drop and was once the low water run before a particularly nasty piece of bedrock "disappeared" from the right channel.

CAUTION - The river pushes left on the entry so beware of drifting off your line and into the steep, nasty, recirculating hole ("SNR Hole") left of the standard line. Between 3.5 and 4.5 feet a powerful "Ledge Hole" forms on the bottom right bank.

48

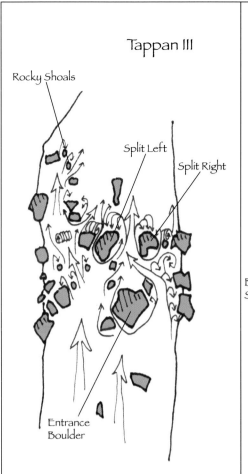

Tappan III

Rocky Shoals
Split Left
Split Right
Entrance Boulder

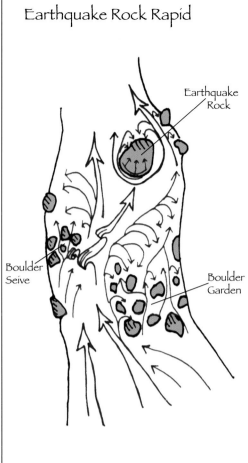

Earthquake Rock Rapid

Earthquake Rock
Boulder Seive
Boulder Garden

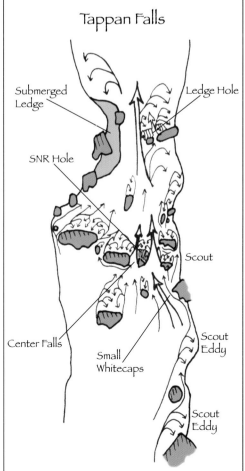

Tappan Falls

Submerged Ledge
Ledge Hole
SNR Hole
Center Falls
Small Whitecaps
Scout
Scout Eddy
Scout Eddy

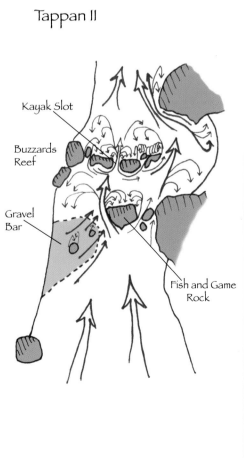

Tappan II

Kayak Slot
Buzzards Reef
Gravel Bar
Fish and Game Rock

Mile 67.8 - Haystack Rapid: Haystack rapid has the most storied history on the river. It has claimed at least two lives in the past 30 years and has seen significant geologic changes. In August of 1997 and again in 1998 rain induced landslides roared down Pole creek, pouring debris into the middle of Haystack Rapid. This made Haystack significantly more difficult at low water. In 2003 Bernard Creek blew out downstream, creating another new rapid. As a result, the lower half of Haystack was submerged. (see G43 on page 90)

High Water – (Class III) Haystack is a formidable place full of massive holes. The safest line is outside left. How Haystack merges with Bernard Creek at high water remains to be seen.

Low Water - (Class II+) As the water drops below 2 feet, the entrance to Haystack rapid becomes tricky. Two runs will get you through. Bounce down the right bank about 15 feet off the edge of the fan. Alternatively, start left of center and float past the right side of a split rock. Run the a small pourover before making a quick pull back to center underneath a shoal of large boulders, and drift into the pool from there. Use proper spacing.

Mile 67.3 - Flying B Airport Camp: (679004E 4981939N) This is a hot and dusty camp on the right bank with little shade. Hike upstream to the Bernard Bridge to access a good swimming hole.

Mile 66.5 - Point of Interest – Flying B Ranch and Store: George Crandell and his wife bought the property in the early thirties. They lived on the river and raised cattle for over 20 years. Pilot A.A. Bennett bought the property and created the membership guest/hunting operation that exists today. Stop in to fill your water jugs and buy ice cream bars at the store.

The Flying B Ranch miraculously escaped destruction during the fire season of 2000. In mid August, a raging firestorm roared down Brush Creek and engulfed the "B" before jumping the river and torching up Warm Springs Creek. They lost only two buildings, but the 80-100 mph winds lifted the Bernard Bridge from its foundation and twisted the steel girders. There is a great photo album of the fires in the store.

Mile 66.5 - Bernard Bridge and Flying B Camp: (678733E 4980747N) The Forest Service identifies a small sand bar camp on the river right beneath the bridge. The cables for the bridge reportedly weighed 1800 pounds and were wrapped around the outside of a plane when flown in.

Mile 65.6 - Point of Interest – Mormon Ranch Cabins: Like many other homesteads and ranches along the river, this one served as a temporary home to many Middle Fork inhabitants. Eventually, the Fish and Game bought out the last private landowner. We used to stop frequently to visit the cabin and cool "spring house" built over a diversion ditch from Warm Springs Creek. Landslides in 1997 clogged the diversion, and the 2000 fires burned the bench and drainage behind the cabins making it a hot and dusty place to visit.

Mile 65.1 - Sheep Creek Camp: (679247E 4979050N) This camp is tucked among the trees at the mouth of Sheep Creek. The large bench upstream has ample tent sites and is good for a game of Frisbee golf. Relax in the shade by the creek on hot August afternoons.

Mile 64.4 - Trail Camp: (679651E 4978040N) Turn right below Aparajo and look for a low, sandy, Ponderosa flat on the right bank. The trail runs through the middle of camp. Don't be surprised if a pack string of mules raises dust at dinnertime. There are plenty of great tent spots among the Ponderosa roots.

Mile 64.2 - Normandy Camp: (679329E 4977699N) Look for an habitable spot on the left bank one mile below Aparajo Rapid.

Mile 63.1 - Aparajo Rapid: One mile below Funston camp and past several large pink granite boulders, the river turns left and slices through Aparajo Canyon. Read and run the class III- wave train at high water and look for kayak surfing opportunities.

Low Water - (Class II+) At the 3 foot level watch out for a sharp boulder disguised in the waves at bottom left. It's embarrassing to get stuck here because you can't get out to push off. For an easy run, follow the current left of this rock. There is a ledgy run right of center over some powerful pour-overs. Watch out for your IK's.

Mile 62.3 - Broken Oar Camp: (678994E 4975516N) Below Funston on the right bank, this small camp sits beneath some great late season chukkar hunting. There is a short walk to a nice overlook downstream.

Mile 62.1 - Funston Camp (Tin Can): (678997E 4975201N) This camp frequently lives up to its name. It has a low kitchen at the upstream high water mark for a shorter carry and a nice beach on the downstream pool. The cliff across the way has another good jump (at your own risk).

Mile 61.8 - Pool Camp: (679337E 4974879N) The main camp sits on a flat bench 15 feet above high water. At low flows, a small beach emerges at the water's edge but offers no shade. There is a great cliff jump across the river (at your own risk).

Mile 61.7 - Point of Interest - Kaufman's Cave: This meager shelter is tucked underneath a cliff wall along the river trail upstream of Pool Camp. A lone Scotsman named Clarence Kaufman built a wooden door to the cave and settled in for several years. He left to visit a doctor and never returned.

Mile 61.3 - Johnny Walker Camp: (679193E 4974207N) This broad grassy bench offers lots of shade on hot summer afternoons. It has a long, flat, and rocky carry across a gravel bar at low water.

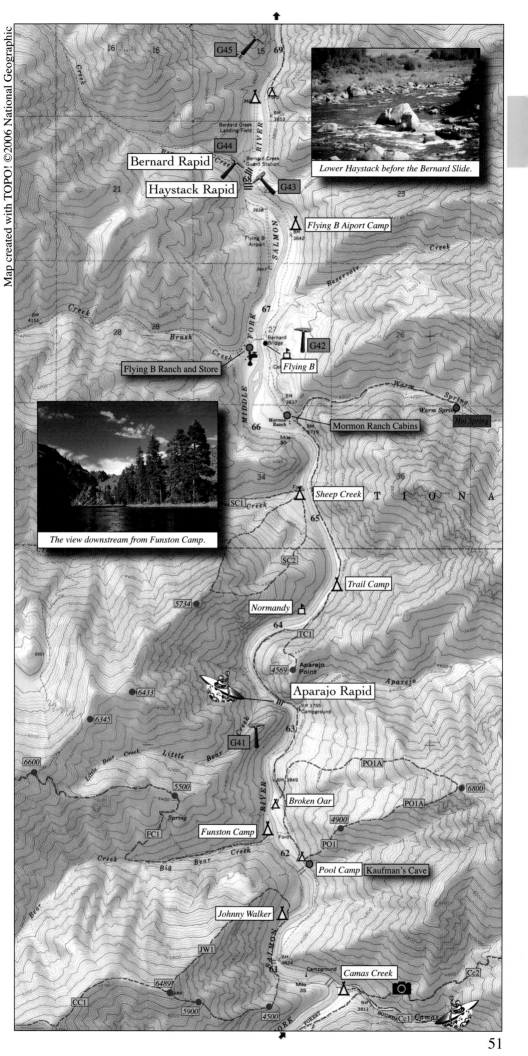

Lower Haystack before the Bernard Slide.

16   16   G45   15   69

Creek

Bernard Rapid

Haystack Rapid

G44

Bernard Creek
Landing/Field

Bernard Creek
Guard Station

68

G43

RIVER

SALMON

Flying B Airport Camp

Flying B
Airport

21

23

Creek

67

27

Brush

28

Creek

MIDDLE

66

Bernard
Bridge

G42

Flying B

Flying B Ranch and Store

Mormon
Ranch

Mormon Ranch Cabins

Warm   Spring

Warm Spring

Hot Spring

FORK

34

Ford

Sheep Creek

SC1   Creek

T   I   O   N   A

65

The view downstream from Funston Camp.

SC2

Trail Camp

5734

Normandy

64

TC1

6433

4569

Aparejo
Point

Aparajo Rapid

Aparejo

6345

Campground

63

G41

Creek

6600

Little

Bear

Creek

PO1A

6800

5500

RIVER

Broken Oar

PO1A

Spring

4900

FC1

Funston Camp

PO1

62

Ford

Big   Bear   Creek

Pool Camp   Kaufman's Cave

Creek

Johnny Walker

JW1

SALMON

61

Camas Creek

Cc2

6489

5900

Campground

Cc1   Camas

4500

FORK   FOREST

CC1

Map created with TOPO! ©2006 National Geographic

Mile 72.7 - Grassy Flat I Camp: (679061E 4989353N) This camp is located on the left bank downstream of Wilson Creek. A spacious grassy flat above high water makes for a roomy camp.

Mile 72.5 - Wilson Creek Camp: (679282E 4989044N) Look for a large sand bar beneath a giant Ponderosa tree on the right bank. Follow the trail downstream to find several tent sites among the trees. Much of the vegetation along this trail burned during the 2000 fires. Walk downstream, and cross Wilson Creek to access the nice gravel beach at the river's edge.

Mile 72.4 - Soldier Creek Rock Dodge:
This long boulder garden starts at the mouth of Soldier Creek and provides some fun hydraulics around 3 feet. It is a fun, navigational challenge at very low water.

Mile 71.7 - Lower Driftwood Rapid:
(Class II) Just below camp the river bends right and presents a fun wave train. This rapid is best around 3 to 4 feet of water.

Mile 71.6 - Driftwood Camp (Table Rock):
(679182E 4987775N): This is large sand bar with numerous large boulders (watch out for bare toes) and great tent sites on the right bank. The hot sunshine bakes down in August, but there are many shade trees.

Mile 71.4 - Driftwood Rapid:
(Class II) This rapid is identified by a huge boulder left of center next to a slightly overhanging cliff at the bottom. At flows between 3 and 4 feet a small hole forms in the middle of the rapid providing a fun hit. Watch your IK's. Run left for a narrow line under the cliff wall.

Mile 71.3 - Little Pine Boulders:
(Class II) Just below Little Pine camp are several huge boulders in the middle of the river. Above 6.5 feet they form waves that are capable of flipping a boat (I speak from personal experience)! As the water drops to 5 feet, two sticky holes can wreak havoc with inattentive boaters. There is plenty of room to avoid them on river left.

Mile 71.2 - Little Pine Camp: (678980E 4987231N) A nice sand bar/bench combination, Little Pine gets early shade in the hot afternoons of August. It accesses the Johnson Point hike and is great a place to mix margaritas.

Mile 71 - Little Pine Rapid:
(Class II) As you exit the Jack Creek pool, the river swings right into a small class II rapid. Look for a steep pour-over hole left of center starting at 4.5 feet. This can be avoided by taking a center run, or it provides a fun hit on a sunny afternoon. Some kayaking surfing can be found here at lower water.

Mile 70.8 - Jack Creek Rapid:
(Class III-) This marks the end of Jack Creek Canyon as the river finishes a long left turn. Read and run at high water. The standard low water line is right of center, though some rafters may seek out a steep hole that forms in the center around 3.5 feet.

Jack Creek Canyon:
The stretch of water between Earthquake Rock and Jack Creek Rapid is punctuated by several class II and III rapids. Shoot whitewater photos from the right bank.
High Water – (Class III) Get ready for a fast and rollicking ride. Watch for a huge wave train that forms on river left above 6 feet. It starts where the cliffs plunge directly into the river and feeds into Jack Creek Rapid. Hit 'em straight or avoid to river right.

Mile 70.5 - Earthquake Rock:
This rapid was created during the 1983 Borah Peak Earthquake, a magnitude 7 that shook Eastern Idaho. A large rock broke loose from the cliff band high on the right wall and splashed into the river. The rapid sits about halfway into the big left turn through Jack Creek Canyon. See page 47 for a diagram and description.

Mile 69.7 - Cold Springs Camp: (678986E 4985460N) This is a small camp on the river right of a large pool. It has great access to the river trail through Jack Creek Canyon.

Mile 69.6 - Cold Springs Creek Wave Train:
Below Bernard Creek, the river points directly at the twin summits of Johnson Point. As you near the end of this straight section, a small rapid leads into the Cold Springs Creek pool.
High Water – (Class III-) There is a significant wave train here around 7 feet. These are fun breaking rollers, but certainly have the potential to flip a boat.
Low Water – (Class II) A read-and-run rapid at low flows. The pool at the bottom is a great place to stop and swim on hot days.

Mile 68.6 - Short Creek Camp: (678784E 4983753N) Pull in on the right bank one half-mile below Bernard Airstrip. The camp sits on a grass and sandy bench behind a row of trees and shrubs. Look for the access trails to determine your landing. There is great canyon photography below this camp

Mile 68.4 - Bernard Camp: (678607E 4983488N) This is a non-descript camp without much shade at the downstream end of the Bernard airstrip.

Mile 67.9 - Bernard Creek Rapid:
(Class III) This rapid was created when Bernard Creek blew out in 2003, sending tons of rocks and debris into the river. *CAUTION* - Due to the nature of the sharp, angular rock in this rapid, the features are erratic and hard to read. The rocks are grabby at low flows. This is not a good rapid to swim. Expect the unexpected (see panoramic photo on page 85)!

While the lines have and will continue to evolve as the river erodes this new deposit, one constant is a large pile of boulders right of center at the top. These form a large hole/wave/rock hazard at various flows. Run the wave train slightly left of center past these rocks. Rafts that get stuck on these rocks at low water present a scary entrapment possibility for IK's.

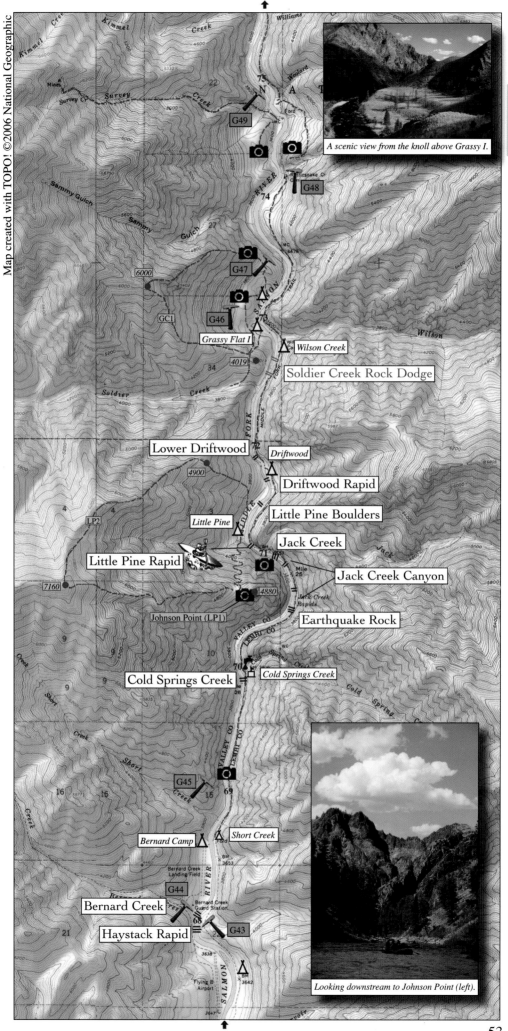

A scenic view from the knoll above Grassy I.

G49

G48

G47

GC1   G46

Grassy Flat I

Wilson Creek

Soldier Creek Rock Dodge

Lower Driftwood   *Driftwood*

Driftwood Rapid

Little Pine Boulders

Little Pine   Jack Creek

Little Pine Rapid   Jack Creek Canyon

Johnson Point (LP1)   Earthquake Rock

Cold Springs Creek   *Cold Springs Creek*

G45

Bernard Camp   *Short Creek*

G44

Bernard Creek

Haystack Rapid   G43

Looking downstream to Johnson Point (left).

Map created with TOPO! ©2006 National Geographic

Mile 78.6 Pine Bluff Camp: (678502E 4997113N): Look for a micro eddy on the left bank just above Cutthroat Rapid. It is a fast pull-in and may be very difficult at high water. The tent sites are on a flood stage sandbar covered in Ponderosa Pine needles.

Mile 77.9 - Last Chance Camp: (678418E 4996051N): This small, rocky bench is perched about 30 feet above the river. A lone Ponderosa shade tree blew down in the nineties and still lies across the bench. Last Chance is more spacious than Big Creek Camp, but I would recommend it only to accommodate Big Creek kayaking or hiking plans.

Mile 77.8 - Big Creek Rapid: (Class II) This a low water boulder garden with two large rocks just below the mouth of Big Creek. I have seen an inattentive boater wrap here, so pay attention if you don't want any embarrassing photos taken.

Mile 77.8 - Big Creek Confluence and Camp: (678346E 4995935N): More like a bivvy spot than a camp, don't plan on sleeping too many here. If you have plans to hike or kayak Big Creek, then this and Last Chance Camp are your two options.

Mile 77.6 - Point of Interest - Waterfall Creek: Pull over to enjoy this spectacular spot in the canyon. Hike downstream to the mouth of Big Creek to stretch your legs and meet the boats. The photo of the falls is best from across the river.

Mile 77.4 - Waterfall Creek Rapid: (Class III) Waterfall Creek Rapid lies just below an expansive gravel bar on river left. The river piles against a small cliff wall on the right bank across from the gravel bar.
High Water – (Class III) At flows above 6 feet most of the gravel bar is covered, so look for the small cliff wall on the right bank. Make a quick right turn below, and enter the rapid. Generally read and run right of center.
Low Water – (Class III-) Several large rocks start to appear bottom center and the right run closes off. Below 2.5 feet enter right, work left, run a pour-over drop, and then pull back right of a large vertical faced boulder on the bottom left. A small sticky hole forms just upstream of this boulder and can flip IK's, so be ready for rescue. Use proper spacing.
CAUTION - The large rock and riffle between the gravel bar and Waterfall Creek is tricky for beginners. Watch for IK's that may tip here and swim through Waterfall Creek.

Mile 77.2 - Fish Camp: (679142E 4995348N): A small sand bar camp at the upstream end of the Waterfall Creek gravel bar.

Mile 76.4 - Pointy Rock Rapid: (Class II+) 1/2 mile below Sam's Hole is another small rapid on a slight left-hand turn. It has a very pointy rock right of center at the bottom. Above 5.5 feet it is possible to run this rather steep hole. I have been catapulted nearly 10 feet above my paddle boat in this one. Below 5 feet avoid this sharp rock to the left.

Mile 75.8 - Sam's Hole: (Class II) The river makes a slight turn to the right about a mile below Fly Camp and narrows into a fun wave train. Hit it straight, or slide off the wave train to the left. There is a large rock dead center that forms a squirrelly hole around 3 feet.

Mile 75.3 - Fly Camp: (679036E 4992955N) This little sandbar will be mostly under water above 6 feet. It has about 4 tent spots, good trail access, and a beautiful waterfall to enjoy.

Mile 75.3 - Kimmel Creek Rapid: (Class II) This is a small rapid with a large rock left of center. Run left to get a close up view of the beautiful Kimmel Creek waterfall. There is a decent kayak surf wave that forms on the right side below 4 feet.

Mile 74.5 - Wollard Wall Rapid: (Class II) This small rapid starts at the end of the Survey Pool and forms a moderate wave train at high water. An inattentive boater, or Sweep boat driver can be swept directly into the wall on river left. The consequences could be dire, so cheat inside right. At low water it is fun to swim in the tail currents of the rapid.

Mile 74.5 - Wollard Camp: (679169E 4991899N): This low grassy bench sits on the right bank just downstream of the towering Survey Cliff wall. There are two landings. Pull in right just downstream of the Survey Wall for an easier unload at high water. The eddy below Wollard Wall rapid is best used at low water. There are several good hikes from this camp.

Mile 74.4 - Survey Wall Rapid: *Extreme Water* - (Class III+) At rare extreme water flows, the s-turn around Survey and Wollard camps is a frightening place. The flooding waters strain through the trees at Survey Camp before crashing headlong into the cliff wall on river right. You have to thread this needle before dealing with the next violent turn downstream in Wollard Wall Rapid.

Mile 74.4 - Survey Camp (Dutch Oven): (679239E 4991705N) Survey is nestled in the high water zone among a Ponderosa Pine grove on the left bank. Numerous sandy tent sites can be found among the gravels. High water above 8 feet will scour this camp clean. There's a great swimming hole for hot afternoons. There are three graves located on the bench above camp.

Mile 74.2 - Point of Interest - Rattlesnake Cave: This overhang tucked behind several trees contains a impressive pictograph panel. There is an interesting geologic contact displayed on the walls (see G48. pgage 91).

Mile 73 - Grassy Flat II Camp: (679139E 4989692N): Located in a rare open section of the Lower Canyon (see G46 on page 91), Grassy Flat II is on the downstream end of the large right hand turn below Wilson Creek. Several large trees, many of which were burned during the 2000 fires, line the bank.

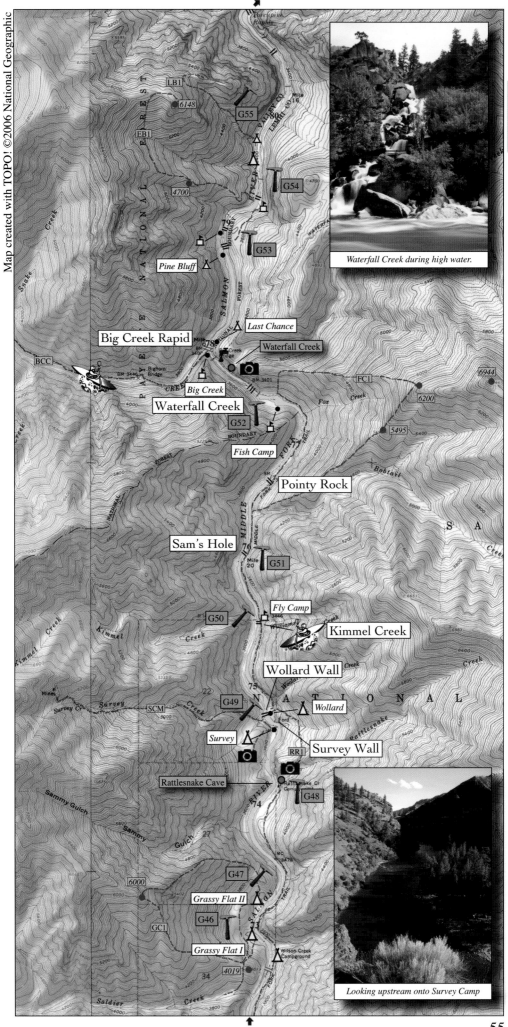

LB1

EB1

6148

G55

G54

4700

G53

Pine Bluff

Last Chance

Waterfall Creek

Big Creek Rapid

BCC

Big Creek

Waterfall Creek

G52

Fish Camp

Pointy Rock

FC1

6944

6200

5495

Sam's Hole

G51

Fly Camp

G50

Kimmel Creek

Wollard Wall

G49

Wollard

Survey

Survey Wall

RR1

Rattlesnake Cave

G48

SCM

G47

Grassy Flat II

G46

Grassy Flat I

GC1

6000

4019

Waterfall Creek during high water.

Looking upstream onto Survey Camp

Mile 82.8 Mist Falls Rapid (Weber): The river turns left below Mist Falls and enters the final rapid in this series. At all levels start right of center and move to the middle of the rapid. At 4 feet a large hole forms at the top center of the rapid with some good kayak surfing potential. Around 3 feet a fun narrow line squeezes among large boulders down the left bank and requires alternate shipping of your oars.

Mile 82.6 Weber (Corkscrew, Redside): See diagram and description on the next page.

Mile 82.4 In Between Rapid: In the middle of the busy wave train between Redside and Weber is a well disguised diagonal wave. At lower flows it is an IK flipper, so be ready for a quick-moving rescue.

Mile 82.2 Redside Rapid (Sevy's Rock, Eagle Rock, Golden Creek Rapid): See diagram and description on the next page.

Mile 82.1 Reside Camp: (678303E 5002101N) This small "honeymoon" camp has only a few tent sites nestled among the rocks. It is, however, the only camp situated in the granite heart of Impassable Canyon. This site accesses some exploratory rock climbing up Golden Creek.

Mile 82 Above Redside Rapid: (Class II) Just upstream of Redside Camp, a small sticky hole forms bottom right below 3 feet. Watch out for IK swimmers as Redside Rapid is not far downstream.

Mile 80.8 Goalpost Rapid (Wave Below Wall Creek): (Class III) A long Class I+ riffle below Wall Creek Rapid leads to this great wave. It forms below 4 feet and keeps getting bigger as the river drops. The best ride is just right of center. This is a great surf wave WITH NO EDDY FEED. The scenery in this part of the canyon is stunning for photos.

Mile 80.6 Wall Creek Rapid (Porcupine): (Class III-) The river makes a sharp right hand turn leaving a large pool at the mouth of Wall creek. A picket fence of large boulders juts in from river left to form the rapid. The tail-waves finish under an overhanging cliff wall on river right. Enter right at all flows to avoid the entry holes/boulders and be ready to pull off the bottom wall.

Mile 80.3 Point of Interest – Veil Cave: A spectacular overhanging waterfall grotto with some great photographic opportunities. This is a popular spot to visit (see hiking description on page 76 for more info).

Mile 80.2 Veil Cave Rapids: (Class II+) At flows above 5 feet, this rapid is a rollicking fun wave train that ends in the Vail Cave pool. At lower flows run down left of center watching for rocks and small holes. There is decent kayak surfing here at low and possibly high flows.

Mile 80 Crystal Pool Riffle: (Class I+) Turn the left corner below Elk Bar, and float alongside a vertical cliff wall. The dramatic granite walls of Impassable Canyon will grow ever higher. As you float out of this Crystal Pool, watch the rocks rise to the surface and slip by underneath your boat. A small rapid follows.

Mile 79.4 Love Bar Camp: (678865E 4998280N) Located just below Elk Bar on the left bank, this camp is a consolation prize compared to the sand bar upstream. It has very little sand or space at high water, but shapes up nicely at lower flows.

Mile 79.3 Elk Bar Camp: (678864E 4998101N) The biggest sand bar on the river, Elk Bar has a stunning downstream view and a lush garden of poison ivy. There's plenty of space at high water, but the low water camp is spectacular. Many groups pass up this gem because it makes for a long last day of floating. The photography from this camp is gorgeous.

Mile 79 Big Pine Rapid: (Class II+) Pass underneath an impressive cliff wall split by several black dikes on river left. The river makes a sharp left turn at Big Pine camp to enter this rapid. There is a large boulder left of center at the bottom that may form a large hole above 7 feet. Run center looking for or avoiding a steep pour-over that forms around 3 feet. Look for a great low-water, eddy-feed, surf wave on the right bank below the rapid.

Mile 79 Big Pine Camp: (678889E 4997606N): This is a nice camp for a small group on the outside right bank below Cutthroat Cove. A sandbar of varying size comes out at low water.

Mile 78.8 Lower Cutthroat Cove Rapid: (Class II) The fun wave train below the Cutthroat Cove pool is best around 3.5 feet. Kayakers should look for a glassy surf at the top starting at 4 feet.

Mile 78.8 Cutthroat Cove Camp: (678466E 499726N): This small, isolated sand bar on the left bank in the pool below Cutthroat Rapid is a low water camp. You can't go anywhere from here.

Mile 78.7 Cutthroat Cove Rapid: Located at the end of the long pool below big creek. The river bends slightly right leading into the rapid.
High Water – (Class III) Run the huge wave train left of center at flows above 6 feet, or slide off into the eddy on the left side. Watch out for the cliff wall on bottom right. There is good surfing potential here at high flows.
Low Water: (Class II) A large thumb rock that sits right of center at the bottom surfaces around 4 feet. It presents a significant wrap hazard, but is easily avoided by following the current left at all low water flows.

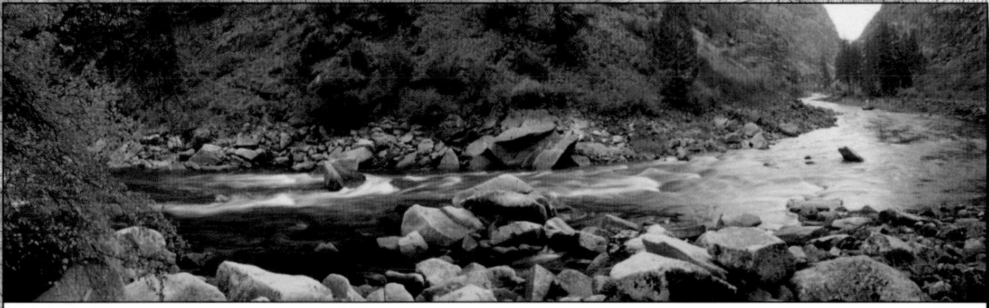

A calm October morning dawns on Redside Rapid (Airplane Rock Sits in the middle of the current left of the photo's center).

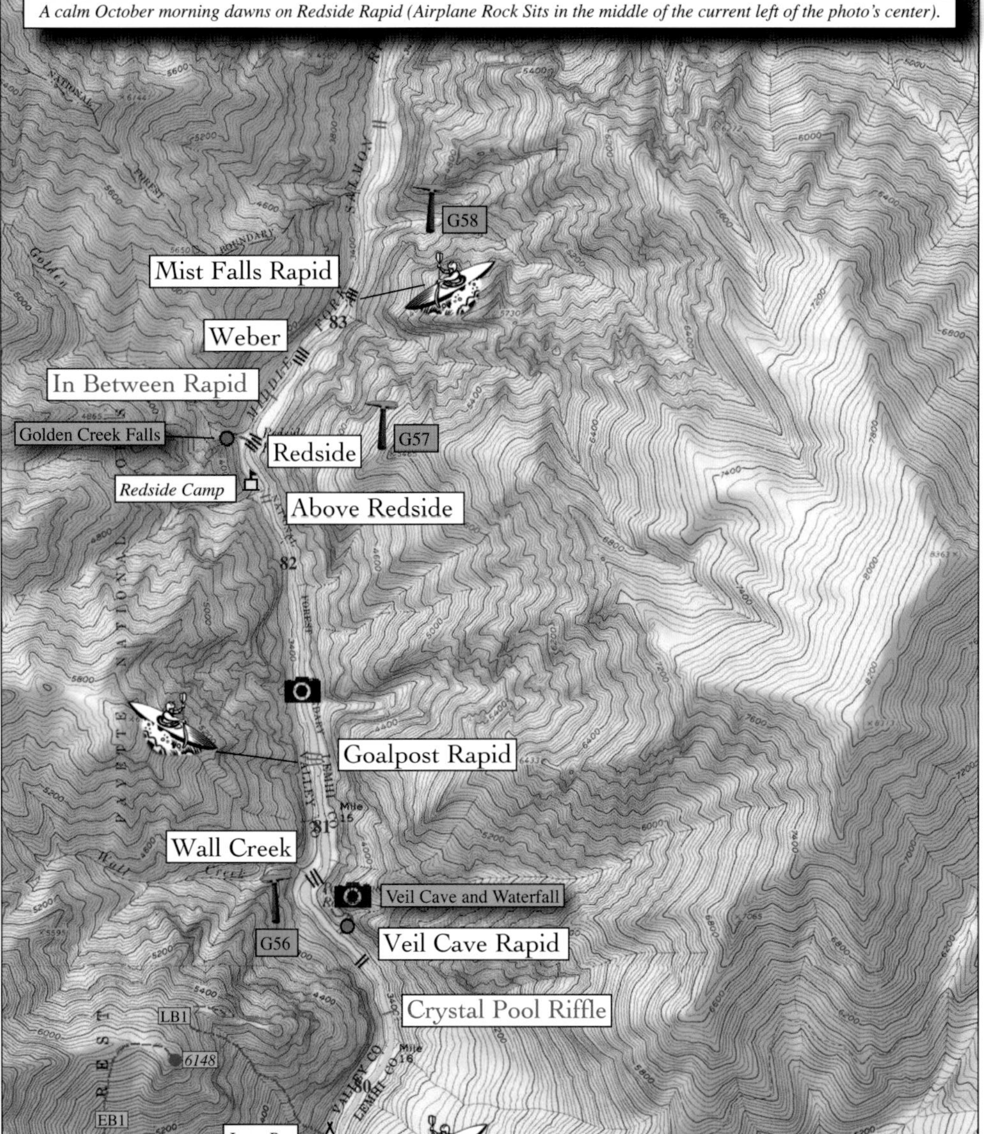

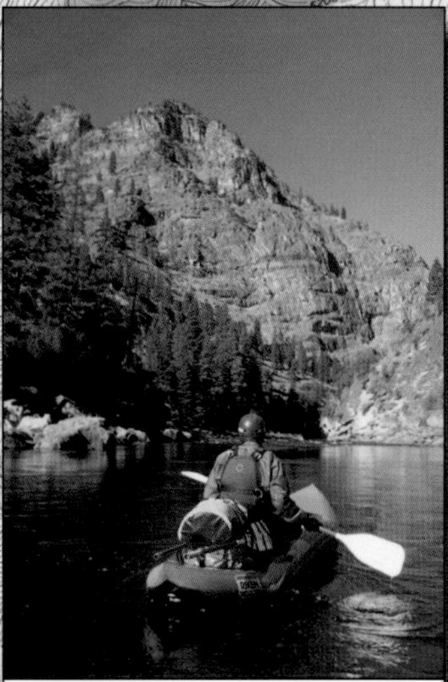

Mile

G58

Mist Falls Rapid

Weber

In Between Rapid

Golden Creek Falls

G57

Redside

Redside Camp

Above Redside

82

Goalpost Rapid

81 · Mile 16

Wall Creek

Veil Cave and Waterfall

G56

Veil Cave Rapid

Crystal Pool Riffle

LB1

6148

EB1

Love Bar

Elk Bar

4700

L. Cutthroat Cove

Big Pine

Big Pine Camp

Cutthroat Cove

Pine Bluff

Cutthroat Cove

Waterfall

Mile 78

Bighorn Bridge

BM 3448

BM 3401

Fox Creek

Drifting into the Impassable Canyon.v

57

Mile 93.2 - Devil'sTooth (Digger Hole): The long straight section below the Devils Molar ends in a boulder choked rapid. Scout from river left.

High Water: (Class III+) Large, boat-flipping holes punctuate the river. The sneak along the left bank is easy until 5 feet. Below 5 feet the large boulders define a center drop that is straightforward and fun.

Low Water: (Class III+ to IV) At flows below 3 feet, making a clean line through Devils Tooth is the most technical challenge on the river. The left side of the channel is defined by the vertical face of a large flat faced "Wall Rock". A jumble of large boulders extends off the right bank, and a huge "Wrap Rock" sits at the bottom right side of the drop. Dead center in this narrow channel is the "Devil's Tooth" itself. Watch for a flat, nasty keeper-hole that forms around 2.5 feet in the main current just below.

At flows around 3 feet the Devil's Tooth forms a steep keeper-hole capable of surfing a fully loaded 18 foot oar boat for several minutes. Around 2 feet this hydraulic diminishes but the drop over the tooth should be avoided. In the 1.5 foot range "the tooth" protrudes enough to hang up a loaded raft. Allow proper spacing.

Left Run (below 4 feet): Coming from right of center, forward push towards the lower 1/3 of the Wall Rock pillow, ship your left oar forward and slip left of the "Devil's Tooth." As the water drops adjust your aim for the downstream end of Wall Rock. You may have to ship your right oar to miss the rocks at the entrance. Keep your boat straight over the drop. This very technical and diffcult run is easier in a paddle boat or sweep.

Right Run (below 2.5 feet): A more conservative and slower run is to back pull into the eddy upstream and right of "Devil's Tooth", drop, and pull left away from "Wrap Rock". Pulling aggressively to the right on the entry move may result in an encounter with 'Wrap Rock."

CAUTION: The steep Devil's Tooth hole/pourover is notorious for tipping IK's and will surf a raft. Swimmers here may drop into the flat keeper hole downstream, where I have seen someone re-circulate 4 times. House Of Rocks is just downstream, so have rescue boats AND throw-bags ready at the bottom.

Mile 82.6 - Weber (Redside/Corckscrew): A second large rapid lays in wait downstream in the middle of the straightaway. Weber rapid is infamous for drowning a passenger and guide on a commercial trip that Dan Rather was on in the late 1970's. The party flipped two boats during extremely high water.

High Water - (Class IV-) Generally run left of center. Between 3 and 4 feet be ready for some surprising hits on bottom left.

Low Water - (Class III-) The holes and rocks become more defined. Punch the "Kayak Flipper" hole on the top left, run a "Second Drop" passing to the left of a "Big Hole" before working to the center at the bottom.

Mile 82.2 - Redside Rapid (Sevy's Rock, Eagle Rock, Golden Creek Rapid): The straight dramatic canyon below Porcupine Rapid makes a 90-degree right turn at the base of some towering granite slabs. Redside Rapid sits on this bend. Scout from river left. This rapid is formed by a picket fence of large boulders that extend off the left bank, the furthest of which is called the "Kaiser's Helmet" Just downstream and right of this picket fence is the huge "Airplane Rock".

High Water - (Class IV-) At flows above 6 feet there is a rumored sneak along the extreme left bank. I prefer to sneak between "Airplane Rock" and the right bank until 3 feet. A center run exploits a weakness right of the "Kaisers Helmet", and rides the left hand pillow off of "Airplane Rock." This is an exposed run between significant boat flipping holes and should not be attempted lightly.

Low Water - (Class II- to III+) Below 3.5 feet the current rushes directly at "Sevy's Rock." Enter right of center and run one of the following lines to avoid the "Sevy's Rock" wrap hazard. 1. Forward push through the left side of the powerful cushion kicking off "Airplane Rock" passing to the right "Sevy's Rock". 2. Back pull into the boiling eddy behind the "Kaisers Helmet" and work left of "Sevys Rock." Below 2.5 feet a small, flat hole forms down and left of "Airplane Rock." It can surf and tip IK's, so be ready with safety.

Mile 22.1 - Pistol Creek Rapid: Once you pass Lake Creek Rapid, Pistol Creek is two quick turns downstream. The river speeds into a tight s-turn veering hard left to avoid bedrock ledges before crashing into the left hand "Pistol Wall". Hike downstream from the Lake Creek debris fan or Huntington Dredge to the scout overlook. There are numerous vantages to photograph Pistol Creek Rapid. Run first and allow 10 to 15 minutes for setup on either side of the river.

High Water – (Class IV) Enter right at the top and aim for the big pillow piling off the "Bedrock Point" right of center. Forward push through the left side of the pillow, and carry momentum past the "Pistol Wall". Essentially you push a straight line through the dollar sign s-turn. Alternatively you can back pull as described for low water.

Low Water – (Class III+) Below 3.5 feet more bedrock ledges emerge creating a well defined S-turn. Pull away from the right hand ledges but watch out for the "Shark Rock" on the river left. Pivot quickly and pull off the left hand wall. 3.5 feet is a difficult stage for this rapid (especially in a Sweep Boat) as the s-turn is well defined with fast current. Use proper spacing.

Weber Rapid

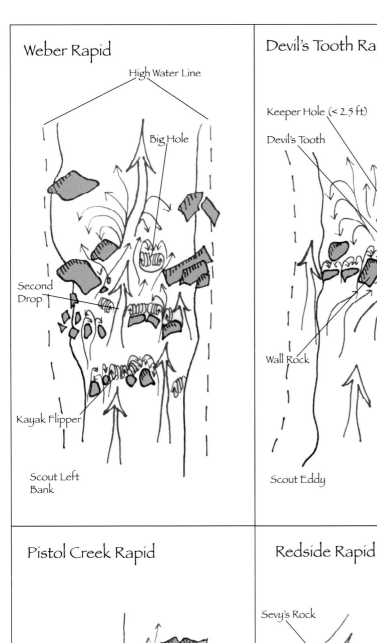

High Water Line

Big Hole

Second Drop

Kayak Flipper

Scout Left Bank

Devil's Tooth Rapid

Rescue Eddy

Keeper Hole (< 2.5 ft)

Devil's Tooth

Wrap Rock

Wall Rock

Scout Eddy

High Water Line

Pistol Creek Rapid

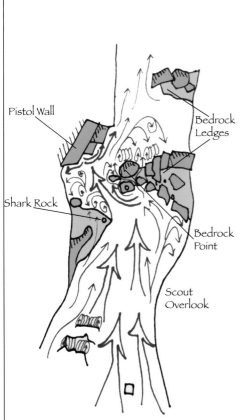

Pistol Wall

Bedrock Ledges

Shark Rock

Bedrock Point

Scout Overlook

Redside Rapid

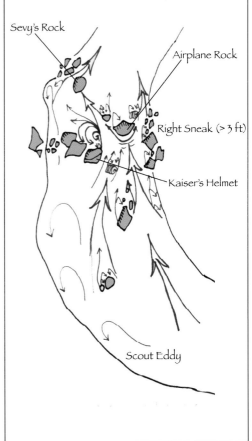

Sevy's Rock

Airplane Rock

Right Sneak (> 3 ft)

Kaiser's Helmet

Scout Eddy

59

Mile 89.6 Cliffside Camp: (682725E 5011611N) The sandbar at Cliffside changes yearly. Sometimes it builds up behind the large rock in camp, while other years there's nary a tent site there. The camp is tight for a full group. Any rock climbers in your group should bring their gear to tackle the splitter crack in the face across the river.

Mile 89.5 Ouzel Camp: (682530E 5011638N): A nice option for a small group, this beach is more spacious at lower flows. Either way, don't expect much privacy. Watch out for the poison ivy behind camp.

Mile 88.6 Tumble Creek Camp: (682072E 5010283N) Tumble Creek camp is located on one of the more dramatic bends of the river. Tent sites cozy up to the steep 50-foot bank and look down onto Lower Cliffside Rapid. At lower flows there may be room for a small kitchen beneath the large boulder at the downstream end of the pull-in. If not, be prepared to carry everything up the steep, rocky trails. On a hot day you can walk up to the base of the rapid and dive in. Drift downstream with your mask and gaze at the beautiful rocks in the riverbed.

Mile 88.5 Lower Clifside Rapid: Start setting up immediately below Upper Cliffside rapid, especially at high water
High Water - (Class III) Hug the inside left cliff wall to avoid large holes in the center. If you get washed right at the entrance, a relatively clean line to the right of center passes huge holes/rocks on both sides.
Low Water - Follow the same inside left line to the far bank at low water to avoid shoals in the bottom center. Don't forget to steal a quick glimpse at the beautiful water-polished cliff wall as you float past.

Mile 88.3 Cradle Creek Camp: (681891E 5009995N): Pull in just below Cliffside on river right, after running safety for your party. At low water a clean gravel bar comes out for an easy kitchen set, but otherwise everything gets carried 30 feet up the trail. Kayakers in your group will appreciate the great surf waves at flows below 3 feet. The eddy, though small, offers a great circular swim at low water (wear your lifejacket)!

Mile 88.3 Cliffside Rapid: You can hear Cliffside from the calm pool below Parrot's Cabin well before you see it.
High Water - (Class II+) The rapid is mostly washed out at high water. Skirt the gravel bar along the right bank to avoid getting pushing into the rock wall.
Low Water - (Class III) As the water drops, a large gravel bar forces an entry left of center. The waves and holes get larger at lower water and peak at about 2.5 feet. There are three significant breaking waves throughout the run. I recommend skirting the first two to the right and hitting the third straight on. At this level, there isn't much current pushing into the "Cheese Grater Wall," but be prepared to move right at the bottom (I find it easier to forward push as I am already set up that way and my oars are clear of the wall). I have seen more botched runs and wall crashes in this rapid than any other. A conservative pull inside along the right bank will avoid everything.

Mile 87.7 Nugget Creek Rapid: (Class II) This is a lengthy rapid below Parrot's Cabin. It reminds me that Cliffside waits below.

Mile 87.6 Parrot's Cabin Camp: (681834E 5008966N): Nugget Creek is a popular spot so day users should pull in at the mouth of the trickling creek. Overnighters will pull in several hundred yards below Earl's winter cabin among large boulders. There are a few tent sites nestled among the boulders and trees back from the river.

Mile 87.5 Point of Interest – Nugget Creek Falls and Parrot's Cabin: Earl Parrot lived a hermits existence at the small cabin here and another above the river in Nugget Creek. His lengthy story is told in "The Middle Fork - A Guide." There is a short walk to a waterfall up Nugget Creek.

Mile 86 Parrot Placer Camp: (680839E 5006710N) Run Parrot Placer Rapid, and pull in to the Grand Canyon sized eddy below. At low water a long narrow sand bar downstream can accommodate more tents. During heavy rain the gully upstream is prone to landslides, so be watchful.

Mile 86 Parrot Placer Rapid: (Class II-) Read and run at all levels.

Mile 84.5 Lightning Strike Camp: (679042E 5005632N): This is a small sandbar camp located on the left bank in the straight-away below Ship Island. There isn't much to do here, so if you have an active group, spend your day exploring upstream. The right turn downstream is very photogenic, so keep your camera ready.

Mile 84.1 Ship Island Camp: (679026E 5005045N) Ship Island is named after the lake perched high in the Bighorn Crags. It has a fast-moving, rocky landing, especially at high water. There is a kitchen landing on the upstream and downstream ends of the pull-in. This is one of my favorite camps for exploratory hiking.

Mile 84 Papoose Camp: (679078E 5004927N): A small sand bar just upstream of the Ship Island pull-in.

Mile 83 Tombstone Rock Rapid: (Class II+) This rapid is located just downstream of a beautiful green and black lichen striped wall on river left. A fun, rolling wave train forms left of center around 3 feet. There is great kayak and paddleboat surfing from a large eddy on river left.

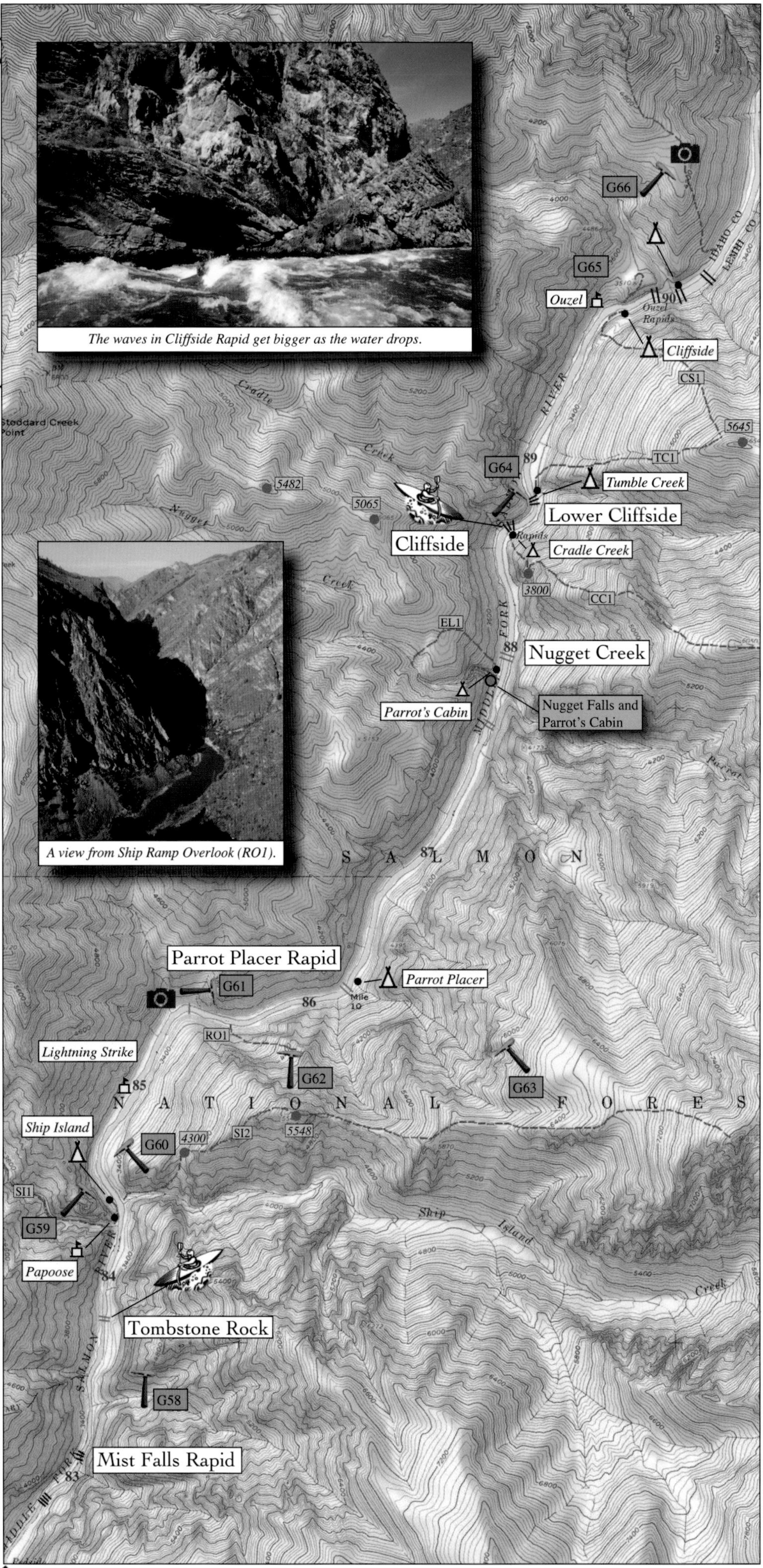
G66
G65
Ouzel
90
Ouzel Rapids
Cliffside
CS1
5645
IDAHO CO
LEMHI CO
RIVER
Stoddard Creek Point
Cradle Creek
89
G64
TC1
Tumble Creek
Lower Cliffside
5482
5065
Nugget Creek
Cliffside
Rapids
Cradle Creek
3800
CC1
EL1
88
Nugget Creek
Parrot's Cabin
Nugget Falls and Parrot's Cabin
MIDDLE FORK
Parrot
S A L M O N
87
Parrot Placer Rapid
G61
Parrot Placer
86
Mile 10
RO1
Lightning Strike
G62
G63
85
N A T I O N A L F O R E S
Ship Island
G60
4300
SI2
5548
SI1
G59
Papoose
84
Ship Island Creek
Tombstone Rock
SALMON
G58
Mist Falls Rapid
83
MIDDLE FORK

The waves in Cliffside Rapid get bigger as the water drops.

A view from Ship Ramp Overlook (RO1).

Mile 93.2 Devil'sTooth: (Class III+ to IV) The long straight section below the Devil's Molar ends in a boulder choked rapid. Scout from river left. See page 59 for a diagram and description)

Mile 93.1 Devil's Molar: (Class II) At the base of several rock spires the river makes a quick jog right against an overhanging cliff wall. The first rapid/rock below is a huge metamorphic boulder I call the "Devil's Molar." It has a concave face that dips slightly upstream. At high flows run either side of the hole. Around 4 feet expert rafters can play on the huge flat pillow recoiling off the concave face upstream. Approach with a cautious backstroke and play at your own risk.

Mile 92.8 Solitude Camp: (685532E 5015236N) A small sandbar camp along the left bank (low water).

Mile 92.7 Below Hancock Riffle: (Class II) Turn the corner left below Hancock and enter a 1/2 mile rapid ending in a pool at the base of impressive rock spires. Kayakers may find surfing at the bottom right of the rapids.

Mile 91.9 Hancock Rapid: Enjoy the beautiful morning reflections before slipping out of the long pool above Hancock. The river bends right starting a long S-turn around the Nolan Creek debris fan before deflecting left around the Roaring Creek fan for a dramatic finish.
Extreme Water – (Class IV-) During a once-in-a-lifetime run above 10 feet, Pete Gibbs recalls the largest waves on the river at the entrance of Hancock. Hug inside left to avoid these boat flippers.
High Water – (Class IV) It's a fun, if slightly washed out, read and run trip at high flows.
Low Water – (Class III+) Hancock is best around 3.5 feet and offers the longest ride on the river. Run the entrance waves, and navigate through the boulders past the mouth of Roaring Creek. Pass right of "Broken Eggshell Rock" before dropping into large waves and holes that punctuate the bottom. Watch for a steep pour-over along the left bank. Below 3 feet a keeper hole forms in the bottom wave train. Starting around 3.5 feet, kayakers should look for a beautiful, wide, catch on the fly surf wave at the very top of the rapid.

Mile 91.5 Below Rubber Rapids: (Class II) Around the corner below Rubber is a long bouncy rapid with two large boulders on the bottom left.

Mile 91.1 Rubber Rapid: This is the largest rapid on the river at most flows. It is on the end of the right hand turn just below Son of Rubber Rapid. Scout from river left between the two rapids. There is great whitewater action in Rubber for photos, but it requires running the rapid first and taking 10 minutes to get set up on river right.
High Water - (Class IV-) The rapid has several huge waves, the most significant of which is a big lateral coming from the left bank. Be sure to pivot your boat and hit it head on, otherwise the chances are good it will roll your boat. It is not always the first wave, so be ready to pivot left mid-rapid. There is a narrow sneak for light boats along the left bank at flows above 6 feet.
Low Water - (Class III to III+) As the water drops, the size and power of the hydraulics diminish, but I have seen rafts flip at 3 feet. Below 3 feet, two submerged boulders emerge on the bottom right of the rapid. There is a channel between these boulders along the bank, so if you get pushed right look for this narrow chute.

Mile 91 Son of Rubber (Vinyl Rapid): (Class II+) Many people mistake this rapid for Rubber. It is a wave train split by a large rock just right of center. Run it left of center at all flows.
CAUTION - There is very little room between this and Rubber. IK swimmers here may get swept through Rubber unless your group is prepared for a quick rescue.

Mile 90.8 Foreplay: (Class II) A long and bouncy rapid with a large boulder on the bottom left. This rapid signals the approach to Rubber. Run it right of center at the bottom.

Mile 90 Otter Bar Camp: (683345E 5011868N) This beautiful sandbar is on the river right just downstream of Stoddard Camp. A large Ponderosa fell across the beach in 2003 and will remain until a significant high water event washes it out.

Mile 89.9 Stoddard Camp: (683104E 5011802N) This spacious camp is situated on a bench 30 feet above the river. The pull-in is swift at all levels, especially at higher flows. If you miss the first trail to camp, there is a second pull-in just 100 yards downstream. There is a beautiful pictograph panel up Stoddard Creek.

Mile 89.8 Ouzel Rapid: (Class II) This long rapid starts as you leave Cliffside Camp. Zigzag between boulders to the mouth of Stoddard Creek. The river in front of Stoddard Camp is littered by several large metamorphic boulders. They form impressive hydraulics at high water. Run along the left bank. Continue through a long bouncy strech that finishes at Otter Bar.

Wall Rock

Devil's Tooth

Setting up to run the left hand slot in Devil's Tooth below 2 feet.

Lining up for the bottom of Hancock Rapid.

G72

99

98

G70

94

Devil's Tooth   House of Rocks
Devil's Molar

G69

Solitude   Below Hancock Riffle

93

Hancock

G67   92   G68

Below Rubber Rapid

Rubber
Son of Rubber

Foreplay   91

G66

Stoddard

Otter Bar

Ouzel

Ouzel

Cliffside

CS1

5645

TC1

89

Taking on Rubber Rapid at 6 Feet.

Mile 98.9 Cache Bar Boat Ramp: The end of the trip! Read the Orientation section for more detailed information about the Cache Bar Take-Out scene.

Mile 98 Cramer Creek Rapid: (Class IV) Look for the horizon line .5 miles above the Cache Bar boat ramp. Scout on river right from the road, and keep your camera handy for action shots. *CAUTION* - This is a large, Grand Canyon-sized rapid and is significantly larger than anything on the Middle Fork at the 3 foot level. It has flipped many boats in its short career, both private and commercial.

"The Dreaded" Cramer Creek used to be a fun, rollicking, deep-water wave train that was a great rapid to swim on hot days. It was altered by a slide in 2002 and will evolve with time, though two large rocks that span in the center of the river should remain in place. Downstream and just off the right bank is another large rounded boulder

High water washes over these center rocks in a fun, big, rolling wave train. Around 4 feet, the two center rocks create a large haystack that builds and breaks irregularly. Watch out! Around 3 feet, a 20-foot-wide monster hole dominates the center of the river. There is a slight weakness in the center for those looking for a challenge.

The standard run is right. Below 3 feet it is tricky to skirt the center hole and still avoid the large rounded boulder just off the downstream bank. At lower water an adventurous but straight-forward line shoots the gap between the two boulders.

Mile 96.7 Stoddard Pack Bridge Rapid: (Class II) After passing the beautiful Stoddard Pack Bridge run a long, rolling wave train that is best at the 3-4 foot level. Look for some holes top right and left.

Mile 96.2 - Confluence Take Out: Congratulations, you successfully navigated the Middle Fork! Take out at the small dirt ramp here, or face Cramer Creek Rapid downstream.

Mile 94.9 Lower Goat Creek Rapid: Round the corner to the right below the mouth of Goat Creek for the last rapid on the river. Downstream, there is a gorgeous view for a photo looking back up the Middle Fork.
High Water - (Class III) At extreme flows (above 8 feet) this rapid extends downstream into some huge breaking waves capable of flipping a raft. Hit 'em straight.
Low Water - (Class II) At flows around 2.5 feet, run along the left bank for the wettest ride. There is a great surf wave with beautiful eddy feed that forms over a bedrock ledge on the bottom right. 4 feet is a good level to try a paddle boat surf, and kayakers should enjoy this last ride.

Mile 94.7 Goat Creek Camp: (687893E 5017213N) This small camp is located on the inside of the bend between Goat Creek Rapids. It is covered at high water.

Mile 94.7 Upper Goat Creek Rapid: (Class II) After passing the BROTMF the river drains into a long calm pool. Looking downstream you will see a blocky ridgeline in the foreground. Take a moment to drift silently through this pool and listen for the descending song of the canyon wren. The rapid you hear downstream is Upper Goat Creek. Read and run this fun wave train at all levels. It is best between 2 to 3 feet and has some good catch-on-the-fly kayak surfing.

Mile 94 Best Rock on the Middle Fork (BROTMF): The straight section below Jump Off is choked by several giant boulders. At flows above 8 feet there are ferocious holes and hydraulics here. At low flows, a humongous flat faced boulder splits the river. Runs are possible on both sides, but the right is recommended. There are strange and powerful currents river left. *BROTMF Geologic Interest* : At flows below 4 feet look at the top right of the second large boulder. There is an interesting geologic feature worth viewing.

Mile 93.8 Jump Off Rapid: This rapid is just below Clamshell rock. Set up on river right.
High Water - (Class III) A straightforward fun ride down the wave trail staying right of center. Watch out for a reflex wave or bedrock ledge hole on the bottom left.
Low Water - (Class III) At extremely low flows (below two feet) this rapid is challenging to navigate cleanly. Two rocks divide the bottom of the rapid into three channels. Enter right, ship your right oar forward, and slip down the right channel. This slot can pinch larger oar boats to a stop. An extremely low water line enters right and pulls hard across the rapid to finish left at the bottom. Allow proper spacing.

Mile 93.7 Clamshell Rock: After a brief lull in the action a giant rock clogs the middle of the narrow canyon. It has a jagged mountainous looking top with a unique downstream formation.
High Water - (Class III) Clamshell rock will be covered around 7.5 feet, possibly forming a huge hole at higher flows. You can run right of the rock until 4 feet.
Low Water – (Class II-) A beautiful, glassy, surf wave forms in the left channel starting around 3 feet. Stop and stay a while in the eddy underneath the Clamshell overhang. Clamshell Rock offers a classic Middle Fork Photo opportunity.

Mile 93.2 House Of Rocks Rapid: Immediately below Devil's Tooth the river is clogged by several house-sized rocks. Look for a bent tree that hangs over the left bank at the entrance. The large rock at the top of the rapid is dangerously undercut!
High Water: (Class IV-) Pull hard left beneath the bent tree to avoid significant hydraulics. Work back to the middle below. A alternate center run weaves among the large holes!
Low Water: (Class III) Take the high water line left, or follow a center channel that weaves among beautiful boulders. Pull through a left slot to avoid dead-ending into the face of the largest rock. *CAUTION*: I won't lead any IK's into the center channel because of a suckhole beneath the right side of the largest downstream boulder.

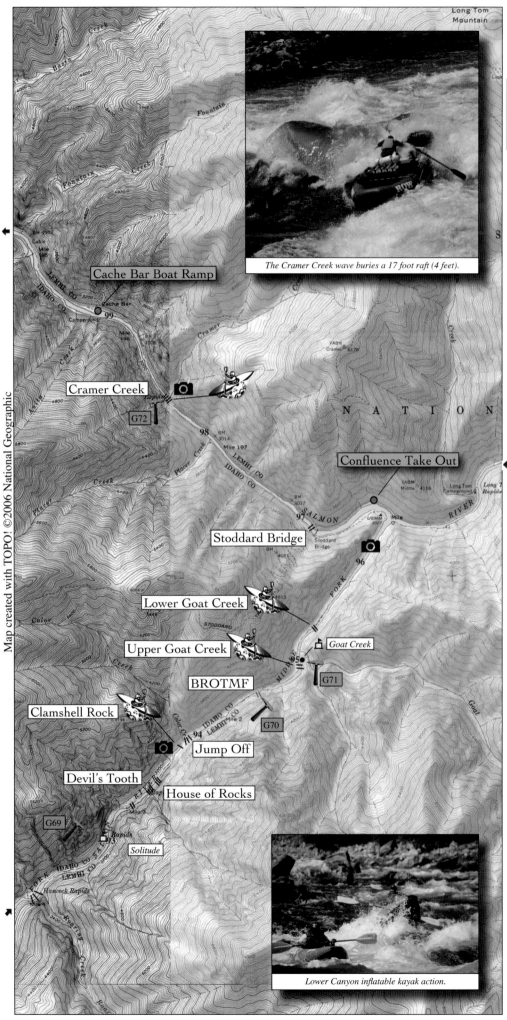

Map created with TOPO! ©2006 National Geographic

The Cramer Creek wave buries a 17 foot raft (4 feet).

Cache Bar Boat Ramp

Cramer Creek

G72

Confluence Take Out

Stoddard Bridge

Lower Goat Creek

Goat Creek

Upper Goat Creek

G71

BROTMF

G70

Clamshell Rock

Jump Off

Devil's Tooth

House of Rocks

G69

Solitude

Lower Canyon inflatable kayak action.

Middle Fork Hiking Descriptions

The following descriptions are intended to provide hikes for all levels of interest. Hiking provides unique a perspective beyond the raft and camp scene that frequently dominates river trips.

Route descriptions, inlcuding class ratings, mileage, and elevation information, are subjective by nature. Some discrepancies may be encountered. I have included several hikes from an extensive "to do" list. If the class rating is followed by a "?" I have never personally hiked the route, but have scouted it from several vantage points. The mileage listed is <u>ONE WAY</u> unless the hike is described as a loop. The elevations provide an approximation of the total vertical gain. Each hike number cooresponds to ones printed on the river maps (in red boxes), and the descriptions are organized by camp or other points of origin. I would appreciate any feedback, especially on the routes I have not personally climbed.

Because the maps are oriented to the river, some of the longer hikes are coverd by two or three map pages. There may even be short sections not shown on any of the topo maps. Keep your fitness level, map reading skills, and route finding capability in mind when choosing any of the more complicated routes. Enjoy the beautiful hiking along the Middle Fork and explore at your own risk.

Mile 0 - Boundary Creek Camp

BC1 - Murph's Hole Scout: (Class 1, .9 miles) Leave the boat ramp from the hand-rail switchback and hike downstream along the river. The trail will fork at a large bedrock/talus outcrop. Stay right on the boaters path and continue along the river to reach a view of Murph's Hole.

BC 2 - Sulphur Creek Trail: (Class 1, 1.8 miles) Follow the river trail from the boat launch staying left when the Murph's Hole scout trail splits right. Climb over glacial moraines and meander through open meadows along the creek.

BC 3- Dagger Falls: (Class 1, .4 miles) From the boat ramp, walk back up the Boundary Creek road and look for a trail marker near the closure gate. Follow this trail across Boundary Creek and enjoy the hike along the steep left bank of the Middle Fork to reach Dagger Falls. There is a bridge across the river upstream of the falls and the trail runs both directions along the right bank. Late June to Mid-July is the best time of year to look for salmon jumping at Dagger Falls. There are great photo opportunities here.

BC 4 - Downed Tree Ridge: (Class 2, 1.7 miles, 1058 ft.) This off-trail hike follows broad ridges through the fire-scarred hills above Boundary Creek. Hundreds of burned and downed trees provide "balance beam" routes among the shrubs. Start at the long-term parking lot and river trailhead. Walk the MF trail a few hundred yards before turning left off-trail before a small saddle. A steep climb to some rock outcrops at 6200 feet provide an expansive view of the glaciated Sulphur Creek Valley. From here follow the main ridge to pt. 6847 and descend to Boundary Creek via the broad SE ridge.

Mile 1 - Teepee Hole Camp

TH1 - Big Soldier Mountain: (Class 1, 3.7 miles 3403 ft.) If you have the time to tackle the steep climb to the summit of Big Soldier Mtn you will be rewarded with spectacular views of the Soldier Lake Peaks to the SE and Greyhound mountain to the East. Row across the Middle Fork at the Teepee Hole pool and walk uphill until you find a trail. Follow it downstream to a right fork that switchbacks 1200 feet straight up a treed, southwest face. The angle eases after gaining a south facing ridge and turns due east at pt. 8111. Turn around here or continue to the saddle at 8800 feet before traversing the ridge north to the Big Soldier Mtn. Lookout. Exploring the Snowstorm Mine and Cabins is an easy alternative for those who don't want the big climb.

Mile 6.8 - Big Bend Camp

Camp Hike: Don't miss the huckleberry patch on the bench 30 feet above the beach. The best pickings are in mid July. Wander upstream to find an impressive old growth Douglas Fir. How many people does it take to encircle the tree?

BB1 - Chutes View: (Class 2?, 1.6 miles, 1965 ft.) It may be possible to explore the north westerly ridge out of the upstream end of camp. It gains an open saddle that looks down on The Chutes Rapid. Gain the ridge and climb 1500 feet to an opening looking into Velvet Creek. Follow the ridge east through intermittent trees, over point 7300, to the saddle on top of the Chutes avalanche path.

Mile 7.3 - Trail Flat Camp

TF1 - Geology Terrace Hike: (Class 1+, .7 miles, 320 ft.) Start by walking downstream on the river trail. Shortly after losing sight of camp, leave the trail and start a gradual climb uphill and left. There are Indian hunting blinds built along the talus base of several distinct flat terraces. The terrace formation is explained in the geology section. Enjoy the quiet woods and wildlife on this gentle hike away from the river.

Mile 9.7 - Boot and Saddle Camps

SC1 - Deer Horn Creek: (Class 1, 3.3 miles, 2701 ft.) Bushwhack to the river trail behind Saddle Camp (Boot Camp hikers will have to wade the river or row a boat across). Head downstream and look for the Deer Horn Creek trail. It climbs beneath some rock outcrops before descending into the creek. Follow this for 3.3 miles to a small lake.

Mile 12.1 - Joe Bump Camp
Camp Hike: Wander the long bench for a historical tour of Joe Bump cabin, placer mining canals and tailings, and Earl "Settrigger" Purcell's gravesite along the trail downstream.

River Trail – Downstream Hot Spring: (Class 1, 1.1 miles) Follow the river trail to a photogenic view looking down on the Sheepeater Island and big avalanche paths further downstream. Continue walking for a soak in the hot springs behind Sheepeater camp.

River Trail – Upstream: (Class 1, <1 mile) A short hike will take you to the swimming hole at the bottom of Powerhouse Rapid (low water). The junction with the Deer Horn Creek trail is 2 miles from camp.

Mile 13.1 - Scout Camp
River Trail – Downstream Hot Spring: (Class 1, .3 miles) Wander behind camp and downstream until you join the main river trail. Follow it to a boulder-studded flat covered in standing water. The hot pools emerge from the hillside halfway down the flat.

Elmer Purcell's grave.

River Trail – Upstream: (Class 1, 1 mile) Follow the trail upstream for a visit to Joe Bump's cabin or to access some good fishing along the left bank of the Middle Fork.

Mile 13.3 - Sheepeater Camp
Camp Hike - Hot Springs: Follow the many feeder trails onto the bench behind camp. Look for the springs against the hillside in the middle of the boulder-studded and boggy flat.

Mile 13.9 - Fire Island Camp
River Trail – Upstream: (Class 1, 1.8 miles) A short .7 mile walk takes you to the Sheepeater hot springs or continue upstream another 1.1 miles to Elmer "Settrigger" Purcell's gravesite and the Joe Bump cabin.

River Trail – Downstream: (Class 1, 1.8 miles) The downstream hike offers a more scenic option than the walk to the Sheepeater Springs. After crossing Lake Creek there is a small climb above the river with a nice view. Continue another mile to the Greyhound pool for some fishing or an afternoon swim.

Mile 15.3 - John's Camp
JC1 - Rocky Point: (Class 2?, .6 miles, 300 ft.) There is a rock outcrop downstream that may provide a short, adventurous hike. There could be a nice view from this vantage point looking both up and down river. Contour uphill and downstream to pt. 5433.

Mile 16.1 - Dome Hole Camp
River Trail - Downstream: (Class 1, 2.3 miles) Scramble uphill until you meet the river trail. Enjoy the pleasant walk downstream 2.3 miles through the Artillery section to the mouth of Rapid River.

DH1 - Dome Creek Ridge: (Class 2-3? 4.2 miles, 4300 ft.) The easterly ridge that defines Dome Creek offers a promising route to the summit of Artillery Dome. After a gradual 600-foot climb, the ridge steepens and turns west. Pick a route up to pt. 6652. From here climb a broad treed shoulder to a clearing at pt. 8009. Enjoy the views and assess your time at this point. The ridge narrows ahead and is likely to become a class 2+ or 3 scramble. 600 feet of climbing gains a trail at 8600 feet which will climb NE to Artillery Dome for a summit experience and spectacular views.

DH1A Point-to-Point: (Class 2-3? 9.4 miles, 4703 feet) A potential option for aggressive and adventurous hikers is to traverse the Middle Fork/Pistol Creek divide and meet a boat at Pistol Creek Camp. This route descends an additional 5.3 miles of open ridgeline through fire scars from the blazes that happened in 2000. Leave Artillery Dome via the north ridge and descend through pt. 8663 and pt. 8354. At pt. 8328 take caution to bear north across the gentle slops above Cannon Creek (head east to descend to Big Snag Camp). At pt. 7549 turn north again staying on the ridge all the way to the valley floor 1/2 mile above Pistol Creek Rapids. The steepest and most difficult section of the descent is the final 1000 feet to the river.

Mile 18.5 - Rapid River Camp
RR1 - Rapid River Trail: (Class 1, 3.7 miles) As Rapid River descends to the Middle Fork it cuts through a scenic rocky canyon. It is 3.7 miles to a campground and trail junction, but the scenic gorge is closer to the river. Kayakers will occasionally run Rapid River to the Middle Fork.

Mile 19.7 - Big Snag Camp
River Trail: (Class 1, .9 miles) Hikers interested

A group enjoys the swimming rock in the Dolly Lake pool.

in geology can hike upstream along flat fill terraces .9 miles to Rapid River or downstream .4 miles to inspect the Cannon Creek debris fan (see the description for G11 on page 86).

BS1 - Pt. 8328 Ridge: (Class 2-3? 2.2 miles, 3449 ft.) Climb the steep, stair master ridge directly behind camp. At 6800 feet the trees open onto a clearing with great views. Turn around or continue to pt. 8328 where is possible to join DH1A for a point-to-point hike to Pistol Creek Camp.

Mile 19.8 - Dolly Lake Camp
Dolly Lake Pool: Walk upstream along the river and climb across the base of the cliff to access the slabs on Dolly Lake pool. To avoid this short technical route, follow the river trail upstream behind the Dolly Lake spire and bushwhack down to the rock slabs on the pool. Bring a life jacket so you can float the river back to camp (see photo previous page).

DL1 - Spire 5306 and Ridge: (Class 2-3? 2.2 miles, 3738 ft.) Above the Dolly Lake spire and further off the river stands Spire 5306. It's summit is 500 feet above Dolly Lake. One possible approach is to follow the river trail upstream and pick a route up the gully that drains into Dolly Lake. Enjoy the views from pt. 5306 or continue up the steep ridge to the east for more a challenging climb.

River Trail – Downstream: (Class 1, 2.3 miles) The river trail downstream crosses a series of 50 foot river terraces that are dotted with large Ponderosa Pine trees. Geology geeks may want to hike the 1.9 miles to the Lake Creek debris fan (see description and photos for G12 on page 86). Continue .4 miles to a great overlook/scout of Pistol Creek Rapid.

Mile 22.2 - Pistol Creek Camp
Camp Hike: Explore the area around the bedrock outcrop left of the rapid. There are a few great spots for cliff jumping (at your own risk), an old bridge foundation, and a small overhanging shelter on the opposite side of the outcrop.

PC1 - Pistol Creek Canyon: (Class 1, 3 miles, 642 ft.) A trail follows Pistol Creek upstream. In 2000 the Little Pistol fire torched the drainage. This hike offers an opportunity to photogaph the natural post-fire, recovery process. Three miles upstream a footbridge crosses Little Pistol Creek. There are hot springs shown on the map a short walk up either drainage from the bridge.

PC2 - Little Soldier Mountain: (Class 1, 6 miles, 3831 ft.) Row across the pool to access the river trail on the right bank. Hike downstream about one-half mile to a junction that turns south and switchbacks up 1500 feet to pt. 6370. Enjoy the views and descend from here or continue to the Little Soldier Mountain Lookout. The full hike is best done with the extra time of a layover day.

Mile 24.9 - Airplane Camp
Camp Hike: Explore the open ponderosa bench both up and downstream from camp. Late May blooms of Arrowleaf Balsamroot and purple Lupine decorate the hillside and flat terraces.

AC1 - Garden Creek Ridge: (Class 2, 1.7 miles, 2240 ft.) Climb the steep ridge directly behind camp to join a pack trail at pt. 6720. Follow this briefly before traversing to pt. 6952 for some great photo opportunities looking downstream onto Pungo Canyon. To avoid the direct climb, walk upstream to Garden Creek. Look for a trail that branches right and switchbacks up the ridge (AC2). Leave the flat shoulder after 6720 and traverse across to Pt. 6952. (this variation is 3.2 miles)

Mile 25.5 - Indian Guard Station Camp
IG1 - Pt. 6952 Direct: (Class 2, 1.1 miles, 2071 ft.) A steep scramble up the hillside behind the ranger station gains 2071 feet over 1.1 miles to a flat shoulder overlook. There are great photo opportunities from pt. 6952 looking towards Pungo Mtn. downstream.

Mile 27 - Indian Creek Camp
IC1 - Point 6203: (Class 1, 3 miles, 1549 ft.) Hike approx one mile up the Indian Creek trail before turning right to switchback up the south facing hillside that leads to point 6203. A great perspective looking down Pungo Canyon will reward the hiker.

Mile 28.2 - Pungo Camp
River Trail – Downstream: (Class 1, 3.4 miles) Follow the river trail downstream from Pungo Camp for an easy and beautiful walk into the narrows of Pungo Canyon. A shorter .9 mile hike is worth the journey for those who want to look at the Orelano Creek Slide (see geology description for G19 on page 87)

Pungo Mine: (Class 1+, .3 miles) Cross Pungo Creek upstream and wander the flats along the river looking for pithouse depressions from the native Sheepeater Indians. Locate tailings piles and three abandoned shafts from the Budell Fluorspar Mine on the hillside. A steep, loose trail leads to the highest of these tunnels approx 200 feet above the river. Bring a headlamp and explore this hardrock mine over 100 feet into the hillside. Foundations for two cabins are tucked up against Pungo Creek.

P1 - Pungo Mountain Loop: (Class 3+ 9.6 miles, 3876) This challenging climb to the flat top of Pungo Mtn. offers expansive views, a summit experience, and a loop hike that goes over and then back through Pungo Canyon. Start by gaining the talus covered ridge immediately behind camp. The crux of the route weaves through steep and rocky terrain in the first thousand feet of the climb. Rock bands can force an exit onto the west face from the main ridge at 5600 feet. Once on the main SW ridge the going is much easier, though steep and without a trail. Enjoy the 360 degree views from the summit. Descend south east towards point 7925 across the top of Teapot Creek. From here follow the broad south ridge over pt. 5232 to the river across from Little Soldier Camp. March the remaining 3.2 miles back upstream to Pungo camp.

Mile 31.7 - Little Soldier Camp
Camp Hike: Little soldier has numerous hiking options, the easiest being a stroll to the rock point behind camp. Follow a camp trail up the left side of Little Soldier Creek and climb to an obscured viewpoint at the top. Finish the walk by circumnavigating the outcrop downstream and looping back into camp. The thimbleberry picking along the bottom of Little Soldier Creek can be great in late July.

LS1 - Patriarch Ponderosa Grove: (Class 1+, 1 mile) Don't pass up this relaxing stroll to a beautiful old growth Ponderosa grove downstream. Walk underneath the rocky point behind camp and traverse uphill to an expansive terrace about 120 feet above the river. There is a small island of rock from which you get a unique view of several trees downed by a microburst in the early 1990's (see photo on page 13) Pick up a faint trail at the downstream end of the bench that climbs slightly higher before turning sharply at Marble Creek rapid. This trail continues to Marble Right Camp.

LS2 - Sunflower Hot Springs: (Class 2, .9 miles, 560 ft.) It is possible to hike over the ridge to Sunflower Hot Springs from Little Soldier. From the island of rock in the Patriarch Ponderosa grove climb the steep hillside to the south east, aiming for the low point in a broad saddle (approx 500 feet). Angle down and right to find the hot springs which bubble from a rock outcrop 50 feet above the river. Please respect any other groups camping or visiting the springs.

Mile 32.4 - Marble Left Camp
River Trail – Downstream: (Class 1, 2.8 miles) Leave camp and follow the trail downstream. It stays high above the river below Marble Right camp and provides some great views looking onto Ski Jump rapid. Continue to Lost Oak Camp and swim across to the hot springs at Sunflower Flat (2 miles) or walk the full 2.8 miles to the bridge at the Middle Fork Lodge

MC1 - Pungo Mountain Hill: (Class 2, .5 miles, 967 ft.) Challenge the youngsters in your group to a race up the hillside directly behind camp. The unofficial record is just over 15 minutes for the 1000 foot climb. The views looking downstream onto Scarface Mtn. are impressive. You can continue up from this broad shoulder to join the Pungo Mountain Loop Hike (P1).

MC2 - Marble Creek Canyon: (Class 1, 2.8 miles, 300 ft.) You can hike up the lush Marble Creek trail for miles. The remains of the Mitchell Ranch are reached after 2.8 miles.

MC3 - Mahoney Lookout West Ridge: (Class 2+, 7.7 miles, 3700 ft.) Cross the Marble Creek Bridge and follow the trail downstream for several hundred yards. Leave the trail, climbing up loose soil right of a small rock outcrop. There is a nice view upstream from the top of these cliffs.
    From here climb the steep, loose hillside above the cliffs for approx. 2000 to pt. 6818. Continue to the Marble Creek/Sunflower Creek divide at pt. 6992. Turn northeast and follow the ridge for another 2 miles and 1000 feet of low angle hiking. Eventually you will meet the trail that leads to the old Mahoney Fire Lookout. Descend your climbing route or drop down the steep NW ridge trail (MC3A) into Marble Creek and follow it back to camp for a 7.7 mile loop.

The Partiarch Ponderosa grove at dawn.

MC3B - A point-to-point opportunity descends east along the ridge that divides Cameron Creek from Mahoney Creek and drops onto the Mahoney Airstrip. From here, follow the river trail downstream to the pool at Mahoney Camp or slightly downstream (higher water) to meet your group.

Mile 32.7 - Marble Right Camp
Patriarch Ponderosa Grove: (Class 1+, .7 miles) climb to the highest of three river terraces behind camp and look for a faint trail that rounds the bend at Marble Creek Rapid. You can follow this to the old growth Ponderosa grove below Little Soldier Camp.

Mile 35.4 - Stateland Left Camp
Camp Hike: There is a great series of old river terraces behind camp and up river. These benches are littered with the bones of elk killed by mountain lions and wolves during the winter. Cross the airstrip road and climb up the steep bank of river cobbles to the well preserved high terraces that sit 280 and 370 feet above the river (see geology photo on page 88).

Hood Ranch Geology Hike: (Class I, 1.1 miles) Walk to the airstrip and pick up a trail at its downstream end. Cross a gully that is washed down to the bedrock then continue to the Hood Ranch cabins. Use the description and map for G24 on page 88 as your guide for exploring the 2003 landslides across the Sunflower Creek alluvial fan.

SL1 - Mahoney Lookout Trail: (Class 1+, 5.7 miles, 3664 ft.) Climb to the 280 and 370 foot terraces upstream of the airstrip. Continue uphill until you join the trail that contours right several miles up to the Mahoney Creek Fire Lookout.

Mile 35.6 - Stateland Right Camp
River Trail: (Class 1, 1 mile) Follow the river trail out of camp and upstream to Thomas Creek (1 mile). Take the trail as far as you like up Thomas Creek.

Mile 36.6 - Hood Ranch Camp
Camp/Geology Hike: Use the description and map for G24 on pg. 86 as your guide for exploring the 2003 landslides across the Sunflower Creek Alluvial Fan.

Mile 38.1 - Upper Jackass Camp
River Trail – Downstream: (Class 1, 1.7 miles) Follow the trail out of camp and onto the flat bench upstream. There are often remains of winter killed game among the trees on this bench. From here, gain the main river trail and follow it downstream for 1.7 miles to some pink bedrock cliffs where you can find indian pictographs. Scramble to the top of the cliffs for a great view onto the river below. Another .3 miles takes you to the Little Loon Creek trail.

Jackass Overlook: (Class 2, .2 miles, 400 ft.) There is a rocky point downstream that provides a great overlook 400 feet above the river. Gain the main trail and follow it downstream past the bubbling waters of Jackass Gulch and underneath the cliff face. Follow several diagonal game trails that lead to the top of the outcrop. The early morning views from this point can be stunning.

JC1 - Jackass Gulch Loop: (Class 2+, 3.7 miles, 2843 ft.) This is one of the better ridgeline loop hikes along the canyon. It offers some easy class III scrambling, expansive views, and finishes just a few hundred yards from the starting point. From Jackass Overlook follow the ridgeline to pt. 6644. Turn slightly right (SW) and continue to a broad shoulder at 7200 feet. Traverse west across the shoulder to the open ridge that divides Jackass Gulch from Little Creek. Descend to pt. 6360 where the ridge splits. Stay right and drop down the NE ridge of Jackass Gulch. The final 300 feet to the river are steep and require some cautious route finding.

Mile 38.7 - Lower Jackass Camp
River Trail: See Upper Jackass hike descriptions for hiking options.

Mile 41.3 - Cougar Creek Ranch
CC1 - Cougar Fire Lookout: (Class 1, 6.7 miles, 3826 ft.) Behind the ranch pick up the Cougar Creek trail. Follow it the 6.7 miles and 3826 feet to the Cougar Lookout.

Mile 42.2 - Mahoney Camp
River Trail: (Class 2, 1/1.7 miles) Gaining the Middle Fork trail on river right is the biggest challenge here. Climb the steep bank 100 feet to a large flat bench behind camp. The trail crosses this flat. Hike downstream 1.7 miles to Fred Paulson's cabin (see Pine Flat hike descriptions) or upstream 1 mile to the Cougar Creek Ranch cabins and trail.

Mahoney Basin: (Class 1+, .3 miles) At moderate to low water it is an easy swim or row across the river. Walk downstream and explore the broad sloping basin on river left. There are remnants of an old cabin and irrigation and farming equipment on the upstream side of the basin.

Mile 43.8 - Pine Flat Camp
Fred Paulson's Cabin: (Class 1, .2 miles) Follow the trail downstream out of camp and up a hill. Fred Paulson's cabin sits at the mouth of the un-named creek nestled among big Douglas Fir trees. The logs used to build this cabin are a testament to Fred's legendary strength.

River Trail – Downstream: (Class 1, 3 miles) Just over a mile downstream from Pine Flat Camp, the river trail comes to Red Bluff creek. The trail will turn up the creek before crossing to climb over 150 feet to the top of the pinkish red wall. There are nice views from here.

Mile 46.8 - Whitie Cox Camp
River Trail – Upstream: (Class 1, 2 miles) Walk up the hillside behind the hot springs to gain the river trail. This hike offers many good river views culminating at the cliff above Red Bluff Creek just short of 2 miles upstream.

Mile 47 - Rock Island Camp
Camp Hike: Stroll to the high bench behind camp and appreciate a depression ringed by rocks that was used by the native Tukuduka peoples, perhaps for spiritual purposes. Downstream Pebble Beach camp (now closed) offers some American Indian history to explore.

River Trail: (Class 1, .9 miles) Follow the trail downstream, across the terrace to the mouth of White Creek. Continue up White Creek Canyon for a longer afternoon stroll.

RI1 - Pt. 6198 Ridge: (Class 2-3? 1.3 miles 2131 feet) The ridge behind camp provides some great views looking upstream. It is possible to follow this ridge all the way to the Mahoney Lookout trail, but pt. 5838 and pt. 6198 are logical places to turn around. They are 1600 and 1800 feet respectively above camp. From pt. 6198 it is over three miles to the junction with the Mahoney Lookout trail.

Mile 48.1 - White Creek Camp

Loon Hot Springs: (Class 1, 3 miles) Most hikers from White Creek choose the long trek to the Loon Creek hot springs (see specific direction to the springs in the Big Loon camp description). The leap off the White Creek bridge into the pool below is exhilerating. Jump at your own risk...

WC1 - White Creek Canyon: (Class 1) Walk downstream to the bridge (or swim the river at low water), cross and head back up to the mouth of White Creek.   The trail continues up White Creek for several miles.

Mile 48.9 - Shelf Camp

Loon Hot Springs: (Class 1, 2.3 miles) Join the hoards of people from White Creek, Shelf, Loon, and Cow Camps that descend upon the Loon Creek hot springs. If the tub is crowded and the afternoon hot, continue up Loon Creek and find solitude among the giant granite boulders and cool pools (low water) in Loon Creek Gorge. (for specifics see the Big Loon hike descriptions).

SH1 - Loon Creek Point: (Class 2, 1.2 miles, 3000 ft.) Climb the stair master like hillside directly behind camp as far as you like. The full 3000 foot climb to Loon Creek Point (7070) is a workout!

SH2 - Bridge to Jack Ridge Loop: (Class 2, 2.3 miles, 2254 ft.) Cross the river (row or use the White Creek Bridge) to access this moderate climb with photogenic upstream views. Climb the left ridge of Bridge Creek to a shoulder 200 feet shy of pt. 6622. Cross east to the SE ridge of Jack Creek and descend to the 4800 foot contour. Snap some scenic photos here. The high speed scree descent past several rock outcrops adds a great finish.

Mile 50.1 - Big Loon Camp

BL1 - Hot Springs Hike: (Class 1, .9 miles) The trail networks accessible from Big Loon Camp afford a variety of hiking opportunities, though most campers opt for the walk to the hot springs for a soak. Follow the trail past the three-sider (outhouse) and parallel to Loon creek. Stay right of Loon Creek Ranch and go through two sets of gates (close them behind you). Cross the bridge over the creek and continue upstream. After .25 miles a wet spot in the trail signals that the hot springs are near. Look for a steep branch leading down to the man made tub on Loon Creek below. Expect to share the springs with hikers from White Creek, Shelf, and Cow Camps.

BL2 - Loon Gorge Hike: (Class 1, 2 miles) If the tub is too crowded, don't pass up the scenic hike upstream. Just 1/4 mile beyond the hot springs, the trail turns right and climbs slowly above Loon Creek Gorge. There is a series of Class IV/V rapids at the bottom of the gorge among gigantic, water polished granite boulders. Most people turn around at the Bennet Creek bridge (2 miles from camp), but the trail continues 22 miles to a dirt road. At low water, there are several steep trails that access the bottom of the creek where you can find beautiful boulders, deep fishing spots and quiet swimming pools. There are unique photo opportunities from every angle in this canyon.

BL3 - Cache Creek: (Class 1?, 3+ miles, 2000 ft.) The maps show a trail behind the Loon Creek Ranch that heads up Cache Creek. Please be polite when passing the cabins. Cache Creek flows through a narrow gorge with some massive granite outcrops upstream.

The stunning Underwater Canyon at low water.

Mile 50.7 - Cow Camp

Camp Hike: Climb the upstream side of the cliff outcrop just behind camp for a great photogenic view. Wander downstream to the next rock outcrop and look for signs of the native Tukuduka along the base. This was once a popular gathering place for these people, probably because of the easy spear fishing at the narrow gorge of Underwater Canyon.

Hospital Bar Hot Spring: (Class 1, 1.8 miles) If the walk to the crowded tub at Loon hot springs is not agreeable, then consider a scenic walk downstream to Hospital Bar. Swim the river from Cave Camp (only recommended at low flows) to access the springs, but be prepared to share with the Hospital Bar campers.

Underwater Canyon: After a short walk downstream, peel off the trail to Underwater Canyon. Bring your goggles for a thrilling swim through the underwater gorge (below 2.5 feet). There are some Indian paintings on the wall across the river, and the view looking upstream from the top of the cliffs above is not to be missed (bring a polarized lens for your camera).

CR1 - Cow Creek Ridge: (Class 2 + steep descent, 5.8 miles, 2674 ft.) Climb Cow Creek's left hand ridge starting directly behind camp. Join the Cow Creek trail or continue hiking up the ridge. Great views looking the up the Middle Fork canyon and into the bowels of the Loon Creek Gorge await. Descend back down the ridge to camp. It is possible to continue through pt. 6310 and cross over Heifer Creek about 200 feet below pt. 6835. Descend the broad northerly ridge to pt. 6122.   From here cross a flat saddle and descend due west from pt. 5920. Exercise caution on the steep descent to the river.

Mile 90 - 52.9 Hospital Bar Camp

Camp Hike: Hospital bar is a large, low lying bench with lots of acreage. There is an overhang/cave upstream of the hot springs to explore. Quiet groves of old growth ponderosas offer a nice atmospher to relax in (when the wind isn't blowing). Improve the hot springs with a large tarp (15' or more) to create one of the best soaks on the river.

HB1- Pt. 6270: (Class II, 2.9 miles, 2427 ft.) The northwest trending ridge behind camp (see top photo on the back cover) climbs above the tall cliffs that tower over the river upstream of the hot springs. You can climb all the way to pt. 6270 but the best photographic views may be lower on the ridge. Descend the way you came, or make a loop by descending the SW ridge to a saddle near pt. 4694. Descend to the river and bushwack to a much needed soak in the Hot Spring.

Mile 53.7 - Cub Creek Camp

CC1 - Bear Point Ridge: (Class II-III? 8+ miles, 4608 ft.) This seldom used camp is the jumping off point for an ambitious point-to-point hike that climbs across the top of Tappan Canyon. Scramble along the river bank downstream and cross the mouth of Cub Creek. Pick a route to the cave on the upstream side of a large cliff wall. Continue up the base of the cliff to gain the left ridge of Cub Creek at pt. 4929. Climb this south facing ridge another 3000 vertical feet through pt. 6020 and pt. 6603 to a shoulder at 7960 just shy of Bear Creek Fire Lookout (it's .66 miles and 700 vertical feet NW to the lookout). Make a 90 degree turn to the right (east) and start heading down the ridge towards the mouth of Camas Creek. The position above Tappan Canyon along the ridge is spectacular.

Descend through pt. 7042 to the end of the main ridge at pt. 6489. There are two route finding decisions of consequence on the descent. Bearing too far south from pt. 6489 will lead down a ridge to the Tappan III Cliff hike (TP1) so to start your descent heading SE. The ridge splits again at 5900 feet. The subtle left ridge (NE) will cliff out in the middle of the Camas face so be sure to turn right (SE) before descending too far below this junction. At 4500 drop left down a north facing blunt grassy ridge to a game trail that leads back to Johnny Walker Camp. You can also continue down the main ridge to the mouth of Camas Creek.

Mile 57 - Grouse Creek Camps

Daisy Tappan's Cabin: Follow the sandy trail through Lower Grouse Camp to visit Daisy Tappan's Cabin. Feel free to go inside. Visitors are welcome by the present owners of the property. Cross the small footbridge over Grouse Creek or wade behind the cabin to explore the old fruit groves on the multi level flats just downstream. Wander to the end of the bench for a view down on Tappan Island.

River Trail – Upstream: (Class I, 2.9 miles) Follow the river trial on a scenic walk upstream through the Grouse Necks (2.9 miles).

River Trail – Downstream: (Class I, 2.5 miles) Hikers not interested in gaining much elevation will enjoy the river trail through Tappan Canyon. Dramatic cliff walled scenery and a Tappan Falls scout are just a few of the highlights. It is 1.5 miles to the falls and 2.5 to the end of the canyon.

UG1- Grouse Creek Ridge – Left: (Class II-III? 4.3 miles, 3926 ft.) Climb the alluvial slopes behind camp up the left side of Grouse Creek. At 4600 feet the ridge will become more defined and turn to the southeast. The view looking upstream onto the Grouse Necks is superb. For a fun class II to III scramble, continue another 800 feet to point 5460. Ambitious hikers with ample time can follow the ridge farther to pt. 6739 and beyond.

LG1 - Grouse Creek Ridge – Right: (Class II, 7.5 miles, 4426 ft.) Cross the creek behind Tappan cabin and climb the broad ridge that divides Grouse Creek from the Middle Fork. The ridge narrows and turns east at approx. 4700 feet where a trail should become obvious (if it hasn't already). The trail will continue up both sides of the ridge offering great downstream views (see photo next page). It is possible to follow this trail to 8326 feet and then turn north on a spur trail that drops back to the Middle Fork at the mouth of Camas Creek (maps not provided).

Mile 58.5 - Tappan Falls

TF1 - Tappan Geology Overlook: (Class II, .6 miles, 600 ft.) For those interested in geology and dramatic above-the-river views this hike is not to be missed. Eddy out below Tappan Falls on the right bank to find the most direct access to the trail about 80 feet off the river. This is the most difficult section of the hike. Follow the river trail upstream just past Tappan I rapid. Start contouring up and left to gain a broad steep ridge. Climb uphill for nearly 400 feet to a rock outcrop at 4600 feet. If heights aren't a personal issue, walk right up to the edge for a dramatic view upstream. See the geology map and description of G38 on page 89 for for info about this unique area.

Mile 59.5 - Tappan IV Pool

TP1 - Tappan III Cliff Overlook: (Class II – III? .4 miles, 920 ft.) The top of the vertical cliff wall that towers over the left bank of Tappan III rapid is accessible via a class II gully up the downstream side. Pull over on the left bank in the pool below Tappan IV. A 900 foot scramble will lead to a saddle at the the contact between the pink Casto Pluton Granite and grey metamorphic rock. Approach the cliff edge with caution.

Mile 60.3 - Camas Creek Camp

Cc1 - Camas Creek Canyon: (Class I, 2.5 miles, 400 ft.) Follow the trail out of camp and up Camas Creek. Cross a bridge and take the right fork to continue up the canyon. There are some horrific looking class V rapids in the first mile of the hike that expert kayakers run at high water. Late season hikers will find cool swimming pools and nice fishing at numerous locations along the creek.

Looking downstream from the Camas Creek shoulder (hike Cc2).

Cc2 -Camas Creek Shoulder: (Class 1+ 1.8 miles, 1858) This relatively short hike offers one of the best scenic overlooks on the river for some great photos. There is a rare vantage looking onto the full horshoe turn of the Middle Fork at the mouth of Camas Creek. Follow the left fork of the trail after crossing the bridge over Camas Creek. After 500 feet, enjoy the stunning view. You can continue another 1358 feet, but the trail eventually fades into the hillside.

Mile 61.3 - Johnny Walker Camp

Camp Hike: Explore the tree lined bank downstream from camp and look for some intricate driftwood piles. As the river turns left, wander up through two or three terrace sequences to a broad flat. Walk the flat upstream to a small cliff band that overlooks camp.

JW1 - Camas Face Loop: (Class 2, 3 miles, 2723 ft.) Johnny Walker accesses a great loop hike that climbs over the big rocky wall facing Camas Creek (see photo above). Begin by gaining the large flat terrace downstream and about 80 feet above the river. Contour steeply up and left to gain a blunt ridge that divides Big Bear Creek from the Middle Fork. Climb 2300 feet to a flat shoulder at 6489 where the Bear Point Ridge hike (CC1) joins this route. There are two route finding decisions of consequence on the descent. Bearing too far south from pt. 6489 will lead down a ridge to the Tappan III Cliff hike (TP1) so start your descent by heading SE. The ridge splits again at 5900 feet. The subtle left ridge (NE) will cliff out in the middle of the Camas face so be sure to turn right (SE) before descending too far below this junction. At 4500 feet drop left down a broad north-facing and grassy ridge to a game trail that leads back to Johnny Walker Camp. It is also possible to continue down the main ridge to the mouth of Camas Creek.

Mile 61.8 - Pool Camp

Kaufman's Cave: (Class 1+) Wander upstream and contour up the first gully on your left. About 300 feet above the river is a small cave that used to be occupied by Clarence Kaufman

River Trail – Downstream: (Class I, 1.3 miles) Follow the river trail downstream 1.3 miles into Aparajo Canyon.

PO1 - Ridge Climb: (Class 2, .6 miles miles, 1000 ft.) There is a short steep hike up the ridge behind Pool Camp that provides a nice view looking both up and downstream. Climb the blunt SW ridge that faces camp to a shoulder at 4900 where it merges with a larger ridge. Retrace the climbing route or continue another 2000 feet up to pt. 6800. Make a loop by descending via the next ridge north (PO1A, 4 miles, 3000 ft.).

Mile 62.1 - Funston Camp

Camp Hike: There is a mysterious ruin of a stone wall in the bushes against the hillside behind camp. It may be possible to wander down the left bank staying above the cliffs that line the river downstream. There are Tukuduka pictographs 3/4 mile downstream among huge pink granite boulders.

FC1 - Bear Creek Lookout Trail: (Class 1, 5.6 miles, 4816 ft.) Follow the trail up Bear Creek. At 4600 feet it will break right and contour up the south facing slopes to a shoulder at 5500 feet. This is a logical turn-around point and there is a great scree-run fall line from this shoulder back into the creek bottom. Ambitious hikers can continue to a set of switchbacks at the head of Little Bear Creek. After 3.3 miles the trail reaches a junction at 6600 feet. The right fork turns NE and descends a ridge before dropping into Sheep Creek. Turn left (west) to continue climbing another 2000 feet to the Bear Creek Point Lookout at 8629 feet and some panoramic views.

Mile 62.3 - Broken Oar Camp

River Trail –Downstream: (Class 1, 1.3 miles) After leaving the large bench behind camp, climb above a cliff band that overlooks the river. Walk out to the edge for a great view. Continue downstream about a mile to the Aparajo Chasm where vertical cliff walls flank the river. The Forest Service blasted the trail through solid rock in this narrow section of the canyon. The

An afternoon view from high on the Grouse Creek ridge (hike LG1).

hiking is easy for another mile and a half downstream.

Aparajo Chasm View: (Class 2, 300 ft.) Wander downstream and gain elevation on a rising contour. After climbing and traversing about 300 feet you should be able to look down into Aparejo chasm.

Mile 64.4 - Trail Camp
Warm Springs Creek Hot Tub: (Class 1, 3 miles 575 ft.)There used to be a wooden hot tub about a mile and a half up Warm Springs Creek. From camp it is a three mile trip (one way) to the springs. This drainage was badly burned during the 2000 fires and the structure may not have survived.

TC1 - Old Aparajo Trail: (Class 1+ .4 miles, 636 ft.) Before the Forest Service blasted a trail through Aparajo chasm, the old trail climbed up and over the cliffs at Aparajo rapid. As you start to climb the Middle Fork trail upstream from camp, look for the old trail that diagonals steeply up the hillside. Follow this to a flat ridge and pt. 4569. Wander around to find an overlook.

Mile 65.1 - Sheep Creek Camp
Camp Hike: Wander up the creek bed among the willows to assess the re-growth after the 2000 fires which burned the creek bottom completely. There are also some small knolls a short distance upstream worth checking out.

SC1 - Sheep Creek Canyon: (Class 1, 1.5 miles, 400 ft.) A trail heads up Sheep Creek for several miles. It is 1.55 miles to the junction with the Bear Creek Lookout Trail.

SC2 - Aparajo Chasm Overlook: (Class 2-3? 2.3 miles, 1948 ft.) For a unique view looking down onto Aparajo chasm, pick a route up the big face behind camp. Climb to just below pt. 5734. Descend the climbing route or a make a loop by dropping down the opposite ridge.

Short Creek Camp
River Trail – Downstream: (Class 2, 2 miles) There is some great scenic hiking along the trail downstream from Short Creek Camp. The canyon walls steepen and close around the river below Haystack Rapid. The hike downstream 2 miles to Earthquake Rock and the beginning of the Jack Creek Rapid series is well worth the trip.

Mile 69.7 - Cold Springs Camp
River Trail – Downstream: (Class 1, 1 mile) The boat trip through Jack Creek Canyon is usually a quick ride punctuated by several rapids. Walking through the canyon from Cold Springs Camp gives a whole different perspective on this narrow turn in the river.

Mile 71.2 - Little Pine Camp
Johnson Point Hike: (Class 1+, 1.2 miles, 1235 ft.) This relatively short but steep climb provides one of the most spectacular views in the lower canyon. Follow a boaters path upstream across the un-named drainage and onto the lightly treed north slope. Climb the switchbacking trail to a saddle and continue up to Johnson Point at 4880 and keep your camera handy for great views in either direction. Much of the trail is visible from camp. There is a small, stone memorial to Eldon Handy in the grass upstream of camp.

LP2 - Johnson Point Loop: (Class 2+, 4.6 miles, 3552 ft.) This is a challenging loop hike that covers a lot of terrain, and is recommended for ambitious hikers only. Walk downstream out of camp and cross the small drainage shown on the map. Climb the steep east face to gain the Soldier Creek/Middle Fork divide ridge on a soft shoulder at 4900 feet. Follow this ridge to the "summit" at 7160 feet (It is 1.2 miles and another 800 feet up the ridge to the Short Creek Fire Lookout). Expansive views looking onto the Flying-B-Ranch are your reward. Descend due east taking caution not to get on the wrong SE ridge. Straight forward route finding through some loose sections will lead to a finish at the Johnson point saddle. Follow the trail down to camp.

Mile 71.6 - Driftwood Camp
Trail Hike – Upstream: (Class 1, .6 miles) The trail climbs above the river across from Little Pine camp before dropping back into Jack Creek Canyon. It is .6 miles to Jack Creek and 1.4 to Earthquake Rock Rapid. The walk through this canyon is sublime.

Tail Hike - Downstream: (Class 1, 2.3 miles) There is a nice cliff overlook just downstream from camp. Climb a short hill and leave the tral as it makes a right turn. Scramble down to a flat clifftop with a nice view downstream. The trail continues .8 miles to Wilson Creek camp and a total of 2.3 miles to Rattlesnake Cave.

Mile 72.5 - Wilson Creek Camp
Trail Hike – Downstream: (Class 1, 1.4 miles) Follow the trail downstream to the pictographs at Rattlsnake Cave. Look for a spur trail that drops left and down to the cave before crossing Rattlesnake Creek. Bring this guide to help interpret the sheep lick sediments and geology around the Grassy Camps (G45 and G46 on page 91).

Mile 72.7 - Grassy Flat I Camp
Camp Hike: Wander the rolling terrain downstream from camp to a high point that looks upstream onto the bend at Wilson Creek. There is a great photo opportunity from here, especially in the spring. See G46 on page 91 for a geologic interpretation of this area.

Soldier Creek Arasta Stone: (Class 1+, .6 miles, 500 feet) Follow one of several human/game trails upstream to pt. 4019. Drop diagonally into Soldier Creek to a small flat in the creek bottom. Though the remains are hard to pick out, an old diversion ditch leads to a worn grinding stone or arasta. The spot is marked by a pick axe head stuck in a burned tree.

GC1 - Grassy Loop Hike: (Class 2-3?, 2.8 miles, 2586 feet) From point 4019 behind camp climb the east facing grassy ridge to the "summit" at 6000 feet. Make a loop by descending the opposite ridge to the NE which should afford some scenic photos looking downstream, especially as you get closer to Grassy II camp. Hold a high contour back upstream to a cold beer in camp.

Mile 73 - Grassy Flat II Camp
Camp Hike: Walk the rolling terrain downstream to a small rock outcrop with good views, or climb to the small "summit" between camps to snap photos looking down on Wilson Creek.

Grassy Loop Hike: reverse the route as described from Grassy I camp.

Mile 74.4 - Survey Creek Camp
Camp Hike: Follow the trail from the downstream end of camp onto the high, grassy expanse uphill. There is a great photographic view from the high point looking upstream. There are three gravesites on this bench.

SCM - Survey Creek Mines: (Class 1+?, 1.8 miles, 2863 feet) The map shows a trail that heads downstream

Dawn risies from the Rattlesnake Cave overlook.

and climbs up Survey Creek to some abandoned mines. Remains of a cabin are hidden in the bushes at the base of the trail. It stands about 3 logs high and is grown over by brush.

Mile 74.5 - Wollard Camp
Trail Hike – Downstream: (Class 1, .7 miles) Follow the river trail downstream past a nice panel of pictographs. The trail stays 100 feet above the river most of the way to Fly Camp.

Survey Overlook: (Class I, short) Follow one of several trails upstream to the top of the wall overlooking Survey camp. The flat top offers an exciting view from the cliff edge, and a great place to enjoy a cold drink.

RR1 - Rattlesnake Ridge Overlook: (Class I, .7 miles, 564 feet) Climb to the Middle Fork trail behind camp (it is easiest to leave camp heading downstream) and follow it on a rising contour upstream. When you reach the high point above Rattlesnake Cave follow the faint trail out the ridge towards the river. The reward is a gorgeous view looking onto the Wollard turns downstream. Bring your camera (see photo above).

Mile 75.3 - Fly Camp
Trail Hike – Downstream: (Class I, 2.5 miles) The hike to Waterfall Creek is nice but feels a bit repetitive on the way back.

FC1 - Crags View Hike: (Class 2-3?, 4.6 miles, 3256 feet) Downstream from Fly Camp, there is a promising loop hike. Walk down to Bobtail creek. Step over the creek and start climbing up the steep ridge to the NE. Follow it through pt. 5495 to a shoulder at 6200 feet. Continue further up to a summit at pt. 6944 for some great views of the Bighorn Crags. Look for Aggipah Mtn to the NNE, Puddin Mtn to the ENE, and Wilson Mtn to the E. Return to the 6200 foot shoulder followed by a quick descent down the west facing ridge towards Waterfall Creek. At 4100 feet the ridge flattens at a broad saddle. Enjoy the view into Waterfall Creek before scree-running plumb line to the river trail below.

Mile 77.8 - Big Creek Camp
BCC - Big Creek Canyon: (Class 1, 4.2 miles, 1259 feet) Hiking up Big Creek links to an extensive trail network along the west side of the Middle Fork. The walk upstream is limited only by time. Hikers interested in fishing will find wonderful trout pools at low water. The Bighorn Bridge 1 mile upstream is a good turn around point. It is another 3.2 miles to the Soldier Bar airstrip and the Big Creek Gorge. The white water is worth the mile long carry upstream for expert hardshell and inflatable kayaks (lower water).

A window-like view from inside the granite Elk Bar cave.

Mile 79 - Big Pine Camp
Geology Hike: For hikers interested in geology, climb the steep hill behind camp to reach the surface of the Cutthroat Landslide Dam. The description of G53 on page 92 provides a good overview of this history.

Mile 79.3 - Elk Bar Camp
Granite Caves and Big Pine Overlook: (Class I+, .4 miles, 200 feet) Walk out of camp and cross the small drainage upstream. Look for a human/game trail that diagonals up the steep hillside. After about 200 feet you will reach a broad flat. Continue walking upstream to find some eroded caves in the granite. Take caution on the pebble covered slabs when climbing to the caves (see photo previous page). Wrap around the hillside downstream from the caves and climb another 200 feet to the top of the cliffs below Cutthroat Cove. Find a comfortable viewpoint and sip a cold drink.

EB1 - Escarpment Ridge: (Class 2-3, 1.8 miles, 2721 feet) Continue up the ridge from the Big Pine overlook. Steep but straightforward hiking leads to a soft shoulder at 4700 feet. Climb to 5400 feet and traverse north into the basin. After working through some steep terrain, gain the open south slopes and climb to the saddle left of point 6148. The view from the point looking down Impassable Canyon is sublime. It may be possible to loop into the Love Bar climb from here.

Mile 79.4 - Love Bar Camp
LB1 - Impassable Canyon View: (Class 2-3, .9 miles, 2248 feet) This straightforward but committing hike leads to dramatic overlooks of the granite heart of the Impassable Canyon. Start directly behind camp and pick a route up the blunt ridge on the hikers right of the drainage behind camp. Take care to stay hikers left of the granite slabs. At about 4400 feet climb left into the gut of the drainage and continue to pick your way to the saddle at 5600 feet. Walk to an overlook and take in the view downstream.

Mile 80.3 - Veil Cave
Veil Cave: (Class II, .4 miles, 400 feet) Climb the boulder field to a well worn path leading into the hikers right side of the cave. You will pass some Indian picotgraphs high on the right cliff wall. Lie on the giant boulder at the base of the falls and look up at the millions of water drops falling from the sky. Curious hikers can follow the trail that leaves the downstream end of the amphitheater via a granite ledge. Step cautiously through the poison ivy that flanks this trail and continue onto the ledge traverse that follows. The trail leads to flat bedrock ledges with a great view onto the river upstream.

> To reach an even more impressive overlook, contour downstream from here until the grassy ledges dead end above Wall Creek Rapid. Take extra caution while crossing the sloping, grassy ledges to an overlook. A misstep could result in a deadly tumble into Wall Creek Rapid. The view downstream is one of the most dramatic in the lower canyon (see photo next page).

Mile 82.1 - Redside Camp
Golden Creek Falls: (Class 2, short) There is a pretty waterfall that glides over the slabs several hundred yards up the creek. What used to be a common side-hike in the 80's, has become obscure with time. The trail that remains is choked by underbrush.

Mile 84.1 - Ship Island Camp
SI1 - Papoose Creek: (Class 2-3 & slippery, 1 mile, 400 feet) Though it seems completely hemmed in by the vertical walls behind camp, confident scramblers are only limited by their imagination at Ship Island Camp. Papoose Creek Canyon offers rugged exploration. Strong hikers with good river shoes are rewarded with isolated grottos, rugged water falls, and a beautiful remote canyon. Closer to the mouth of the canyon there are cool pools to dip in, a short waterfall to scramble behind, and a ramp that leads to an overhanging cave and overlook. CAUTION - Papoose canyon is rugged, loose, and slippery. Explore and hike at your own risk.

Ramp Behind Camp: (Class IV, 300 feet) If the ramp that diagonals up the vertical wall behind camp looks intriguing to you, then give it a try. It is a relatively easy, though horribly exposed scramble with a few climbing moves added in for good measure. The ramp accesses a notch with great views downstream.   It is crucial to note landmarks so you can find your way back onto the initial ramp.

SI2 - Ship Island Ridge: (Class 2-3, 2.1 miles, 3047 feet) At low water take a kayak across the downstream end of the Papoose pool to the mouth of Ship Island creek. The right ridge of the Ship Island drainage drops precipitously into the creek from a broad open slope. There are two ways to gain this slope. 1. Scramble up the hikers left side of the creek and gain the ridge via the steep gully that tops out at 4300 feet (class III+). 2. Walk downstream from Ship Island Creek, across the broad terrace and pick a route that skirts the cliff bands guarding access to the open face. Follow the edge of the open slope until your legs tire. Pt. 5548 may be impassable, but the view downstream is impressive. If you can skirt pt. 5548 and cross the rocky ridge to the east it is smooth sailing another 3000 vertical feet to the top of the granite spires that look down onto Ship Island Lake in the Bighorn Crags.

Mile 85.6 - Turn Below Ship Island
RO1 - Ship Ramp Overlook: (Class II, .4 miles, 1090 feet) The 90 degree right hand turn below Ship Island greets boaters with one of the most spectacular vistas on the river. Broad open ramps climb out of the river with dramatic vertical drops on the downstream side. Pull over on

river right at the talus pile that pours off the most obvious ramp (see 2nd photo on the back cover). You can gain the ramp by climbing this pile and following numerous sheep trails to a beautiful overlook at 4300 feet.

Mile 87.6 - Parrot's Cabin Camp

Nugget Creek Falls: (Class I+, .2 miles, 300 feet) Pull into the eddy at the mouth of Nugget Creek and follow the well traveled trail up the cool canyon. After 10 to 15 minutes the canyon opens into a wide grotto with a 150 foot waterfall cascading through a slot.

EL1 - Earl's Ladders: (Class 2+, .6 miles, 1191 feet) About halfway up the Nugget Falls trail, look for a spur that climbs out of the creek onto a sloping ramp downstream. There are remnants of the ladders Earl Parrot built to help him negotiate the small cliff bands that punctuate the 1000 climb out of the canyon. These ladders are not necessary to climb the face, but it is fun to look for the scattered remnants of wood and nails. Climb to a broad shoulder at 4400 feet. Earl's cabin was burned in a fire but you may be able to find the foundation somewhere in the bottom of Nugget Creek. Hikers looking for a good view of the Bighorn Crags can climb NW up the left ridge of Nugget Creek towards point 5065. It is possible to climb through pt. 5482 all the way to Stoddard Creek Point at 7400 feet.

Mile 88.3 - Cradle Creek Camp

CC1 - Canyon Wall Hike: (Class 2, 1.9 miles, 2853 feet) Walk to the upstream end of the tent sites and contour uphill to gain a broad ridge behind camp. Follow this through some small rock bands to an upstream overlook at 3800 feet. Continue as long as your legs hold out, though the ridge at 5400 feet will likely get jagged enough to force a retreat.

Mile 88.6 - Tumble Creek

TC1 - Tumble Slope: (Class 2, 1 mile, 2278 feet) Walk out of camp and across the rugged terrace downstream. Continue until you can pick a route through the rock bands guarding access to the broad slope above. Once through these obstacles, continue hiking along the dramatic precipice into Tumble Creek. At 4600 feet you will enter a ghostly forest of burned and bleached Mountain Mahogany. There is a good overlook at pt. 5645. It may be possible to summit Goat Mountain in the Big Horn Crags from here.

Mile 89.6 - Cliffside Camp

Cliffside Crack: (Class V, 5.9+ fingers to hands) Navigate a boat into the corner of the cliff wall at the base of a striking crack that climbs directly out of the water. This variable width crack is 5.9+ with a crux about 20 feet off the water. Bring slings to build a new rappel station as the ones on top are several years old. There are more potential routes along the cliff walls on the river left.

Pt. 3510: (Class 2, .2 miles, 280 feet) Swim or row across the river and climb the sloping ramp that cuts through the cliff bands downstream. The view looking upstream from pt. 3510 is beautiful.

CS1 - Spire Behind Camp: (Class 2-3? 1 mile, 2290 feet) There is a small rock spire above camp for a possible scrambling adventure. Work your way upstream (watch out for the poison ivy) and find a reasonable route to the summit. You can continue up the broad face SE of camp for over 2000 feet to join the Tumble Slope hike at pt. 5645.

Mile 89.9 - Stoddard Camp

Pictograph Panel: Follow a trail up Stoddard Creek to the best panel of Indian pictographs on the river. Oil from you skin will degrade the paintings so please don't touch!

Stoddard/Otter Overlook: (Class 2-3?, 1000 feet) Scramble up the gully downstream of Stoddard Creek. Negotiate several steep rock bands and climb to the top of the cliffs overlooking Otter Bar. For a longer hike and a view down onto Rubber Rapid, climb the easy ridge to a lone tree at 4200. There is a broad flat bench here. By continuing up the ridge, it may be possible to reach the Stoddard Trail just past pt. 6106

Mile 90 - Otter Bar

Stoddard/Otter Overlook: (Class II 300 feet) cross the river and scramble to the base of the cliffs. Follow a ledge system through the wall to gain the left side of the cliff. Climb this to an overlook that looks down on both camps. Continue as described in the Stoddard section.

A stunning view of Impassable Canyon from the Veil Cave overlook.

The Geologic History of the Middle Fork

Floating through miles of a remote river canyon offers a unique way to see the landscape. The waters of the Middle Fork of the Salmon lead rafters through different eclgical regions, beginning in lush high-alpine forests and finishing at the bottom of a dramatic desert canyon. Rivers also provide a look into the geologic past by cleaving the landscape and exposing the bedrock underbelly of the region.

Geology is difficult for many people to fathom because of the huge scope of time involved in the processes. If you squeezed the 4 billion years of the Earth's geologic history into a 365-day calendar, Jan. 1st would represent the formation of the planet and midnight on Dec 31st would represent modern day. In this hypothetical geologic year, the formation of the bedrock along the Middle Fork began around Nov. 15th while humans do not enter the scene until the last second of the New Year.

This huge difference between geologic and human history can make it difficult to fully understand the massive amount of time involved in the formation of the Middle Fork landscape. Even within this geologic continuum, events occur on different timescales. The mountains of Central Idaho were built over a span of 100 million years. The Middle Fork has been carving its canyon for only the last 2 million, and much of the modern landscape we see along the river has been shaped by events happening in the last 15 – 20,000 years. Humans have been evolving on the globe for the past 20,000 years.

Just as a photographer looks at the world through the perspective of different lenses, geologists have to adjust their perspective to conceptualize the history of our planet. In order to better understand the geology of the Middle Fork, it is useful to view this history through different "lenses" of time.

The Wide-Angle View – 100 to 2 Million Years Ago: Bedrock Origins of the Middle Fork

If you view geologic history through a wide-angle lens the small details are difficult to pick out, but the big picture of Plate Tectonics dominates the scene. Like giant plates of ice floating on the polar seas, geologists believe that pieces of Earth's crust float and collide on the liquid core of our planet. This tectonic dance began 4 billion years ago and continues today. The configuration of continents we recognize on modern maps is thought to be only the most current version. The formation of the bedrock geology surrounding the Middle Fork began 100 million year ago (mya) and is best understood by viewing events through a wide-angle lens of time.

Before the Rocky Mountains
Land in western Idaho at the beginning of this period was beach-front property. The North American Plate had yet to accumulate the crustal pieces that that would become Oregon and Washington. Most of Idaho was a flat coastal plain bordering the Pacific Ocean. The state was covered in layers of sediment eroding from an ancient mountain range to the east. These "Belt Sediments" were over 8,000 feet thick and composed of layered rock ranging from mudstone and shale, to sandstone and limestone (Figs. 1 & 2).

Subduction Begins
Starting roughly 100 mya Tectonic forces began pushing the North American Plate to the west. At the same time, the expansion of the Pacific Ocean Basin forced it's associated plate eastward. This opposing directional movement caused the thinner, denser Pacific plate to slide underneath the more buoyant North America and dive into the molten Asthenosphere below. The leading

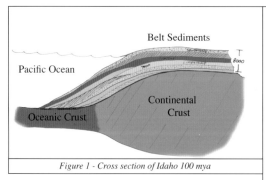

Figure 1 - Cross section of Idaho 100 mya

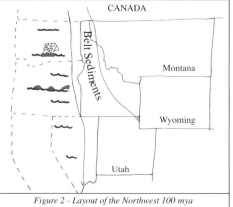

Figure 2 - Layout of the Northwest 100 mya

edge of the Pacific Plate melted in the hot underbelly of the earth sending large plumes of molten rock rising towards the surface. This magma would eventually solidify into huge regions of granite know as the "Idaho Batholith" (Fig. 3 next page).

As the superheated mass of liquid granite rose to the surface it bulged the earth's crust and formed a series of "Island Arc" subduction volcanoes much like Mt. St. Helens (Fig. 4 next page). When the rising mass of magma encountered the underside of the "Belt Sediments" it spread

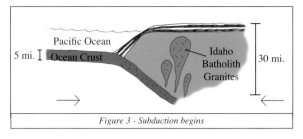

Figure 3 - Subduction begins

underneath the sedimentary layers of ordered rock. Over time, large masses of the "Belt Sediments" slid east and west on this lubricating magma creating additional mountain ranges. You can see examples of this folded and twisted sedimentary rock in the Pioneer, White Cloud, and Lost River Mountains in east central Idaho.

In addition, a zone of intense "contact metamorphism" occurred where the plumes of hot magma came into contact with the colder continental rocks above. The rocks in this zone were super-heated enough to behave like silly putty. As massive forces squeezed and pulled at the malleable rock, the individual minerals aligned in bands of dark and light layers (Fig. 5. This "Gneissic Banding" was further folded, twisted, and injected with magma to create a zone of fascinating metamorphic rock along the boundaries of the Idaho Batholith granites).

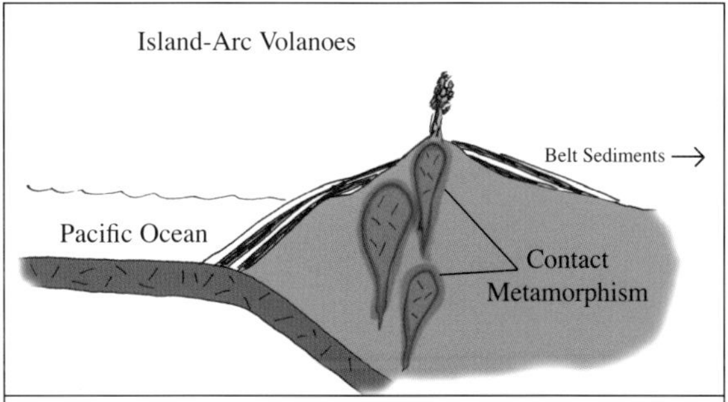

New Land and Continent-Continent Collisions

As millions of years slipped by, the Pacific Plate continued its journey beneath North America feeding the rising magma, contact metamorphism, and associated surface volcanoes. (Fig. 6A) Eventually a small piece of continental crust, much like a pre-historic Hawaiian Island, was carried into the subduction zone (Fig. 6B)

Figure 4 - Rising magma and island-Arc volacnoes

This collision of two crustal plates, 30 miles thick created a massive mountain range that stretched up and down central and western Idaho. The Himalaya Mtns in Asia are a modern day equivalent of such a continent/continent collision. These new mountains rose tens of thousands of feet high and jumbled the western "Belt sediments" with additional sedimentary and volcatnic rocks dragged into the collision. This event

Figure 5 - Gneissic banding

represents the birth of the Rocky Mountains and joined what would become the eastern portions of Oregon and Washington to North American Plate (Fig. 6C).

Sometime after the birth of the Rocky Mountains, roughly 50 mya, another magma chamber rose beneath Idaho. This magma resulted in a massive series of volcanic explosions and related deposits in the eastern part of the state. Although the "Challis Volcanics" (as these rocks are called) don't crop out along the Middle Fork the "Casto Pluton" granites associated with this second magma intrusion are prominently displayed along the river (Fig. 7).

Figure 6A - 6C - Collison sequence

The bedrock exposed along the Middle Fork is a result of this 100 million years of geologic history. The significant exposures seen along the river are Idaho Batholith and Casto Pluton granites, associated contact metamorphism, and the jumbled and broken pieces of the Belt Sediments.

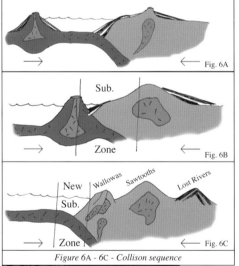

Figure 7 - Casto pluto outcrop

The Zoomed-In View – 2 Million to 20,000 Years Ago: Mountainous Glaciers and their Relation to Middle Fork Geology

Re-focus the perspective of time. The wide angle movement of the global plates is nearly imperceptible, but when you zoom-in it is possible to watch global sheets of ice advance and recede, glaciers cut magnificent cirques in the high mountains, and rivers carve into the landscape.

Geologists estimate that the big-picture layout of the Northwest and Central Idaho were tectonically established about 2 mya. The subduction boundary shifted west and formed new island arc volcanoes along the modern Pacific coast. The continent looked much like it does today (Fig. 8). This is the setting in which the long-term erosion of Central Idaho by icy mountainous glaciers and hungry river systems occurred.

The Cycle of Ice Ages

Early studies of seafloor sediment and oxygen isotopes provided evidence of repetitive ice ages. While the story unfolded at the bottom of the ocean, the actual cause of this cycle is related to the eccentricity, oscillation, and wobble in the orbital paths of the earth and sun. Over time, the net solar gain or loss to earth's atmosphere has been the driving force behind global ice ages. The icy periods lasted for roughly 20,000 years of a 100,000 year cycle. In the past 2 million years, rivers of ice have engulfed Central Idaho's mountains an estimated 15 to 20 times.

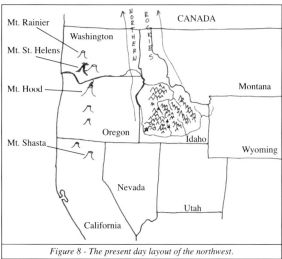

Figure 8 - The present day layout of the northwest.

Did Glaciers Carve The Middle Fork?

So how does this apply to Middle Fork geology? During an ice age, the mountains of Central Idaho above 6000 feet contained smaller glaciers that carved the beautiful high mountain cirques found in the Sawtooths, White Cloud Mountains, and in the Big Horn Crags (just east of the Middle Fork's Impassable Canyon). The elevation of the put-in at Boundary Creek is 5800 feet, so the canyons of the Middle Fork were NOT directly carved by these rivers of ice.

One mountainous glacier did reached the Middle Fork at the mouth of Sulphur Creek (see explanation for G1 on pp. 85), but the ice <u>did not turn down the main canyon</u>. While ice age glaciers did not physically carve the river's canyon, the outwash sediment they brought into the system did have a significant effect on the overall hydrologic balance of the river.

A Balancing Act

Rivers are much more than water flowing downhill. Rivers are liquid highways that move broken pieces of mountain to the ocean. The main stem of the Middle Fork is fed by many tributaries, which in turn are fed by hundreds of smaller streams. Draw in it's entirety, the watershed of the Middle Fork looks less like a single ribbon of blue winding through mountains, but rather a dendritic system of veins, ready to catch and transport every boulder, pebble, or speck of sand that enters it's water (Fig. 9).

Rivers are in a constant balancing act between the volume of water in the system and the "bed load" of sediment they are forced to carry. This is represented by the scales in Fig. 10. An increase of sediment on one side of the scale requires an increase of water to effectively move the additional bed load downstream. Conversely, if the volume of water increases without an addition of sediment, the system will have extra energy to carve material from it's own river bed.

The long term results of this balancing act will result in one of three scenarios:

<u>Aggradation</u> or filling will occur when there is more sediment coming into the system than the available water has the ability to transport. The canyon will be filled with the extra alluvial sediment (Fig. 11 next page).

<u>Degradation</u> or incision by the river will occur if there is greater water volume than the available bed load requires for transport. In this scenario the river will carve deeper into its canyon (Fig. 12 next page).

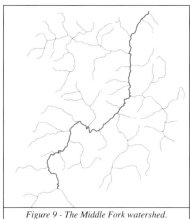

Figure 9 - The Middle Fork watershed.

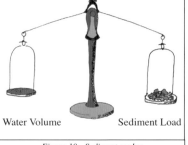

Water Volume   Sediment Load

Figure 10 - Sediment scales

<u>Lateral erosion</u> occurs when the water volume and bed load are in equilibrium. The river will neither fill nor carve into it's channel, but does erode laterally over time (Fig. 13 next page).

Glacial Fill and Inter-Glacial Erosion

While the mountainous glaciers surrounding the Middle Fork were not actually carving the canyon, they were crushing and grinding rock in the upper elevations of the system. These glaciers were capable of moving an enormous amount of sediment on their icy backs, depositing tons of rock, gravel, sand and silt into the Middle Fork watershed. During these glacial episodes, the river had to deal with a massive influx of sediment, far greater than the existing water volume could transport. There was no option but to leave some of it behind, and the Middle Fork began to fill its canyon (Fig. 14).

For 20,000 years (the typical duration of an ice age) the Middle Fork filled its canyon with sediment creating a wide flat valley bottom with braided stream channels This historical river was probably very similar to modern day glacial river valleys in Alaska.

During the intervening non-glacial period (80,000 years) the scales tipped again, this time in favor of the water volume. The Middle Fork began the arduous task of removing tons of accumulated sand and gravel fill (Fig. 15). It eventually reached the bedrock floor of the canyon and, during the remainder of the interglacial period, continued to deepen the canyon through the process of incision (Fig. 16).

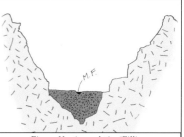

Figure 11 - Aggradation/Filling

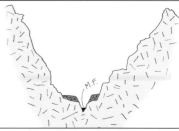

Figure 12 - Degradation/Incision

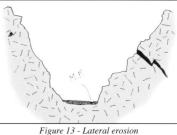

Figure 13 - Lateral erosion

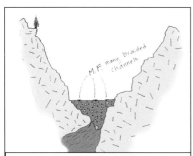

Figure 14 - Glacial filling

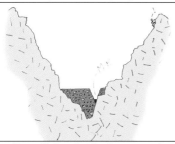

Figure 15 - Interglacial sediment removal

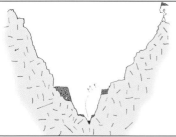

Figure 16 - Interglacial incision

Figure 17 - Second glacial filling

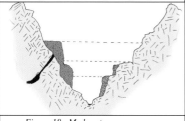

Figure 18 - Modern terrace sequence

Like clockwork, the glaciers returned filling the Middle Fork with a second round of sediment, but not quite as high as the previous level (Fig. 17). A period of interglacial removal and further down-cutting followed. This cycle occurred between ten and twenty times in the last two million years. The repetitive history of glacial filling followed by degradation and incision can be seen today in the remnant terraces that remain in the canyon (Fig. 18).

So How Deep Has the River Carved?

My thesis research in 1995 and '96, included mapping the elevations of the terraces along the Middle Fork. There are multiple terrace elevations that likely correspond to a period of glacial filling. The most obvious was a 50-foot surface that graded from the mouth of the Sulpher Creek Glacier into the Middle Fork during the last ice age (15-20,000 ya). The highest fill surface lies 360 feet above the river and is roughly 600,000 years old. Using this terrace sequence as evidence, it appears that Middle Fork has carved at least 360 feet into the massive canyon in the last 600,000 years.

While there are a few possible locations where higher terraces may be preserved, the older glacial fill surfaces have likely eroded into the river as the deepening canyon also widened and eroded laterally. Geologists estimate that the Middle Fork has been flowing in its present course for 2 million years. Though we have yet to find higher terraces to project river incision rates beyond our 360 foot/600,000 year estimate, the landscape of the canyon supports a theory of further incision by the river.

After years of hiking in the Impassable Canyon, I begin to notice a significant break in the steep terrain about 1000 feet above the river. If we triple of our proposed river incision rate to extend through the 2 million year history of the Middle Fork the river would have carved 1080 feet into the canyon over the past 1.8 million years. The photograph in Fig. 19 supports this theory, showing an abrupt change in steepness at this 1000-foot level. During its 2 million year history the waters of the Middle Fork have probably carved over 1000 feet into the lanscape forming a magnificent and narrow inner gorge.

Figure 19 - The 1000 foot break in Impassable Canyon.

The Close-Up View - 20,000 Years Ago to Present Day: Post Glacial Erosion Events.

Re-Focus again, this time look at the geologic history through a close-up lens. Humans enter the landscape in this perspective, but we get only hints of Tectonic activity. Single earthquakes, nearly insignificant in the bigger geologic picture, shake our world. Glaciers from the last ice age have receded. While the dance of colliding plates fades into the background, the close-up view focuses on very recent geology. The erosion of the Middle Fork canyon continues through landslide events that are very dramatic in our human perspective.

Sheep Licks and Lake Sediments
During a research trip in 1995 we stopped to investigate a curious exposure of sediment in the side of a gravel terrace below Wilson Creek. The local inhabitants, Rocky Mountain Big Horn Sheep, frequently clawed at this deposit and we were curious to find out why. Upon closer investigation, we discovered a series of fine-grained "marls", or calcium-carbonate deposits. (Fig. 21 next page)

Frequently, microscopic underwater organisms will use carbon di-oxide from the atmosphere to build a calcium carbonate shell. A "marl" is formed when these critters die and settle to the bottom and form a layer of calcium on the lake bed. The Sheep are attracted to this necessary mineral. Lactating mothers need calcium to produce milk, and both sexes need calcium for the development of their characteristic horns (Fig. 20).

While the sheep were no doubt happy to find this rich calcium deposit, we were curious how a sediment typical of still water lakes could be found in a terrace of river gravels. The answer lay nearly six miles downriver at Cutthroat Cove.

Figure 20 - Big horn sheep

A Catastrophic Collapse
The 200 foot terrace on the right bank above Cutthroat Cove is not like other fill terraces found throughout the rest of the canyon. Rather, it was probably formed by an historical landslide that inundated 15 miles of the Middle Fork and backed lake waters upstream to Bernard Camp. The Cutthroat Cove terrace is carpeted with large boulders and other debris, not the smaller river deposited cobbles normally found on fill terraces. There also appears to be an old river bed cutting across the surface which may be an early drainage channel.

The Cutthroat Cove landslide was likely the result of a massive rock-fall from a high granite escarpment on river left (Figs. 22 and 23 next page). It completely dammed the river and probably took several years to fill. This provided the still waters required for the marl deposition upstream, and enough time for the river to fill the reservoir with it's bed-load of sediment. Radio carbon analysis of the marl date the landslide event at 12,000 years ago. (see description for G46 on page 91). It may have taken decades for the river to work through this giant dam in the river channel.

We discovered a second deposit of marls exposed by sheep on the right bank below Elk Bar. This provided evidence of yet another massive landslide damming event. This dramatic rock-fall probably tumbled into Weber Rapid from high on the righ bank. The marl associated with this second event was dated at 1800 years old (see G57 on page 92).

Figure 21 - Calcium carbonate marl sediments

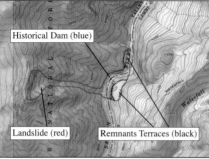

Historical Dam (blue)

Landslide (red)   Remnants Terraces (black)

Figure 22 - Cutthroat Cove slide map

Figure 23 - Photo showing the slide path and dam site.

Modern Middle Fork Geologic History

When floating through the granite gorge of Impassable Canyon, it is easy to imagine how a massive rock-fall could dam the river. Though significant, these two geologic events were certainly not the only ones to alter the Middle Fork. Members of an early float trip in 1936 encountered a series of landslides that occurred during a massive rainstorm that summer. The largest slide started on the west face of Big Soldier Mtn. Heavy rains lubricated the soil and the steep, saturated hillside released a slurry of water, mud, and boulders that thundered into the river.

The debris entered the Middle Fork from an unnamed canyon on river right creating the somewhat mis-named "Sulphur Slide" Rapid. A member of the expedition, Charles Kelly wrote, "Floated down a mile to the rock slide. It came down (with several others) last summer in a cloudburst. Had dammed up the river for a quarter mile. Slide was 20 feet deep. The stream was full of big rocks. We lined the boats down." In 70 years, the Middle Fork has managed to move and re-distribute much of that sediment but a challenging rapid remains (see description for G4 of page 85 for more details).

The debris flow that created Sulphur Slide Rapid was one of several in the summer of 1936. Eroded debris fans, grown over with trees and shrubs can be found on the right bank below Sheepeater Camp, at the mouth of Mortar Creek, and downstream at Cannon Creek Rapid (see G11 on page 86). The journals of early rafters make note of encountering and lining their boats around several of these slides in the late 1930s and early 40s.

There were very few river altering landslides between the 1936 and 1997. The Mortar Creek fire in 1979 burned across many tributaries, but the only events related to these fires are the small slide on Scarface Mountain and a moderate landslide from Greyhound Creek (see G7 and G24 pages 86 and 88). The Borah Peak Earthquake in 1983 shook the walls of Jack Creek Canyon loosening a large chunk of the cliff wall into the river. The resulting rapid dubbed "Earthquake Rock" is now a class significant class III.

Post 1997 Landslide Events

In August of 1997 a massive thundershower over the Flying B ranch triggered a landslide that altered Haystack Rapid. Since then, geologic events have created no fewer than 10 new rapids on the Middle Fork and Main Salmon Rivers (Fig. 24). What follows is a timetable of the events and a summary of the geologic activity that has occurred in the last nine years. There are more detailed descriptions for several of these slides included in the mile-by-mile geology notes.

August 1997 – Pole Creek (Haystack):

A huge thunderstorm focused its intensity in the Flying B Ranch area. There were many small slides on the hills surrounding the ranch including several that blocked the airstrip road. Large fans entered the river at the mouth of Reservoir Creek and Pole Creek, forever altering Haystack Rapid. Several smaller

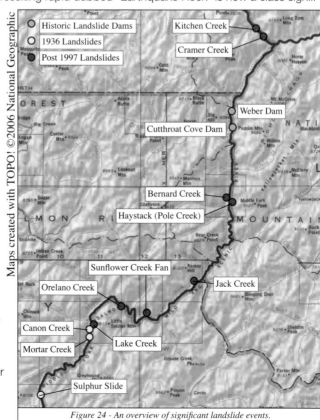

Maps created with TOPO! ©2006 National Geographic

○ Historic Landslide Dams
○ 1936 Landslides
□ Post 1997 Landslides

Kitchen Creek
Cramer Creek
Weber Dam
Cutthroat Cove Dam
Bernard Creek
Haystack (Pole Creek)
Sunflower Creek Fan
Jack Creek
Orelano Creek
Canon Creek
Lake Creek
Mortar Creek
Sulphur Slide

Figure 24 - An overview of significant landslide events.

"gully washers" impacted the Middle Fork trail along the right bank in Jack Creek Canyon. Pole Creek blew out again sometime during the summer of 1999 and added to the pile of debris on the right bank fan (see G43 on page 90).

August 2000 – Middle Fork Fires: A summer of intense fire swept across the Middle Fork region in 2000. The Little Pistol Creek fire burned significant acreage along the river from Lake Creek to the Indian Creek Bridge (Fig. 25). Another fire complex swept down on the Flying B Ranch burning Brush and Bernard Creek drainages. The river corridor was blackened from Aparajo Rapid to Grassy II Camp (mile 63 to 73). Several of these fire impacted slopes would eventually spill debris into the Middle Fork.

Figure 25 - Fire damage up Pistol Creek.

August 2001 - Lake Creek: The Lake Creek (near Pistol Creek) blow out was the first landslide related to the fires in 2000. It happened in Mid-August when most river parties were launching from Indian Creek. Boaters reported a mandatory portage around the log choked channel on river left.

July 2002 – Orelano Creek, Jack Creek, and Kitchen Creek: An intense storm system struck the Middle Fork region in mid July of 2002. The resulting landslide in Pungo Canyon (Fig. 27), dubbed "Oreo," included a nasty log pile that caught a few boaters off guard with an undercut trap. Fortunately, the logs washed clear with high water the following spring.

Several small slides happened on the granitic hillsides around Loon Creek. Jack Creek on river left spilled several huge boulders into the channel creating a new class II+ rapid upstream of Loon Creek. Kitchen Creek, just a few miles below the Cache Bar takeout on the Main Salmon sent a large debris fan into the river. It backed a temporary lake upstream for several miles inundating a good portion of the Cache Bar Take-Out.

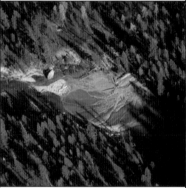
Figure 26 - The 2nd Lake Creek fan.

Late July 2002 – Sunflower Creek: Later that summer in July, another storm struck the Little Creek area. Nearly every drainage on the open, granitic hillsides above Hood Ranch Hot Springs spilled debris onto the existing alluvial fan. Car sized boulders were carried several hundred yards, and smaller material washed into a broad fan along the river left bank. The slide re-routed Sunflower hot spring, drying up the old pipe that was used as a shower.

Summer 2003 – Lake Creek #2: A second debris flow occurred again at Lake Creek sometime in 2003 spreading a similar fan into the river and forcing the current into a narrow left hand channel with a fun class II+ wave train (Fig. 26). We sank to our knees in un-solidified muck when scouting the rapid for the fist time. It takes several days for the slurry of water, silt, sand, and gravel to settle enough to make a walkable surface.

July - August 2003 – Cramer Creek Fire and Landslide: The Cramer Creek Fire burned along the Main Salmon in July of 2003. There were temporary closures of the Cache Bar road, and several vehicles were shuttled to safety as the flames marched towards Cache Bar. Two Heli-Tac fire fighters were killed while fighting the blaze along its upper flanks. Later that summer, rain on the fresh fire scars caused Cramer Creek to flash-flood into the Middle Fork. The augmented Cramer Creek Rapid is a significant Class IV that continues to catch boaters by suprise.

Figure 27 - Orelano Creek fan (note the boats in the lower left).

August 2003 – Bernard Creek: After six seasons of yearly evolution, boaters were finally figuring out how to run the "New Haystack" Rapid. Then, in 2003 heavy rain on the fire denuded hillsides above Bernard Creek resulted in a new fan just downstream. The slack water behind this new slide drowned over half of Haystack Rapid. Bernard Creek and Haystack will continue to evolve as high water re-arranges this rock choked turn in the river (Fig. 28)

The same storm system triggered three

more landslides along the Main Salmon just upstream of the Middle Fork confluence. The Cache Bar road was closed for nearly two days trapping several river parties in the canyon. The Forest Service delivered fresh water and military issue Meals Ready to Eat (MREs) to the stranded floaters. Several veteran river guides struggled with the complicated packaging and small print on the directions.

There has been much discussion amongst boaters on the Middle Fork regarding this recent string of geologic events. Some are excited to watch the change, while others dread the technical dangers presented by the new rapids. Thirty-year veterans comment that they can't remember such drastic changes happening during their early tenure. Is this recent series of landslides related to long or short term climate change, or just a random sampling of natural processes? Only time will tell. Meanwhile, the Middle Fork continues flowing without comment.

Figure 28 - Bernard Creek rapid in 2003. Note the similar fan deposits covered in green vegetation on the left bank downstream.

Mile by Mile Geology Descriptions

The following descriptions of geologic points of interest correspond to the geology hammer icons on the river maps. The sites are labeled in numeric order starting with G1 at Sulphur Creek. These descriptions often refer to events described in the previous section on the Geologic History of the Middle Fork.

G1 - Mile 2.3 – Glacial Topography: The outlet of Sulphur Creek is small compared to the width of this glacially carved canyon. During the last ice age glaciers advanced down Sulphur Creek and butted against the Middle Fork. There are several lateral and terminal moraine deposits that mark the extent of the glacial advance (Fig. 1 red lines). On the northern side of the drainage near Prospect Creek are several "Kettle Lakes." These are created when buried chunks of ice melt, leaving a depression in the topography that fills with surface water.

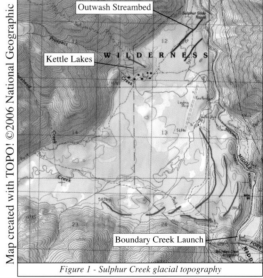

Figure 1 - Sulphur Creek glacial topography

A glacial outwash streambed is marked by the blue lines on Fig. 1. This surface lies approximately 50 feet above the current river level but represents maximum height of alluvial filling during the last glacial episode. These and other 50 foot terraces are 15-20,000 years old.

G2 - Mile 2.5 – Avalanche Input: A steep avalanche path enters the river on the right bank above Pinball Rapid. Frequent winter slides introduce debris into the river channel and may partially explain the abundance of rocks downstream.

G3 - Mile 2.7 – Glacial Boulders: There is a curious deposit of large gravel boulders along the left bank below Pinball. The linear pile of gravel stands 15 to 20 feet above the river. The orderly deposition may be linked to the glacial outwash activity at the mouth of Sulphur Creek Canyon.

G4 - Mile 3.1 – Sulphur Slide Rapid: Suphur slide rapid was created in 1936 by a major landslide on the right bank. The rapid was portaged by many early rafting parties in the 1930's and 40's. Much of the slide debris has been re-deposited downstream forming a shallow island of mixed rounded and angular sediment.

G5 - Mile 6.4 – Terrace and Overburden: The glacial fill terraces along the Middle Fork have a tenuous existence in the steep sections of the canyon. They are easily washed away with long term erosion and widening of the canyon. Or, as in the example along the right bank just above Big Bend Camp, they are covered with "overburden" sediments that fall from the hillsides above.

G6 - Mile 11 – Freeze Thaw Erosion: As you turn the long corner around the mouth of Deer Horn Creek, there are many jagged granodiorite cliffs. The upper Middle Fork experiences significant erosion from freeze-thaw expansion during the winter and early spring. The fractured rock accumulates in the large "talus" slopes at the base of the cliffs.

G7 - Mile 15.8 - Deflection Erosion: Greyhound Creek experienced a landslide sometime after the Mortar Creek fire in 1979. Most of the deposition has been transported downstream (creating some tricky low water maneuvering) but you can see where the initial force of the deflected current eroded into the left bank exposing river gravels from a glacial fill terrace.

G8 - Mile 18.9 – Sediment Island: Mortar Creek Island splits the river into two channels. As you float past the downstream end, look for a deposit of angular, blocky rock along the left bank. Mortar Creek was one of several drainages that experienced a debris-flow during the 1936 storm cycle. The original deposit may have created a temporary lake that filled with sediment. As the river cut through the dam and backfilled sediment, stranded high water logs would have diverted water to either side preserving a small island in the middle of the river. Shrubs and trees add stability to the island helping maintain its foothold in the center of the channel.

G9 - Mile 19 – Glacial Fill Exposure: The eroded right bank below Mortar Creek Island exposes a thick cross section of river-rounded alluvial fill. The top of the deposit (you can't see it from below) represents the vertical extent of the last glacial filling episode 15-20,000 years ago. The introduction of the Mortar Creek slide upstream may be responsible for the extensive erosion into the right bank.

G10 - Mile 19.7 – Dolly Lake Gravel Sort: Variable flow rates have a sorting effect on the bed load of a river. When a fast moving current slows, the heaviest sediment will be deposited first while lighter gravels can travel further downstream. When entering Dolly Lake Pool at low water look along the right bank to see this progression from large to small gravels.

G11 - Mile 20 - Cannon Creek Blowout: There is a fun little geologic mystery to solve between Dolly Lake and Cannon Creek Rapid. As you float through this section take note of the following clues: 1. Several large, standing dead trees on the right bank at Dolly Lake Camp. 2. A significant accumulation of mid sized gravels and micro terraces along the right bank below the camp. 3. A heavily eroded bank of glacial fill to the right of Cannon Creek Rapid. 4. A vertical deposit of sharp, angular sediment on the left bank just below Cannon Creek. 5. A large log-jam and gravel island downstream.

Cannon Creek blew out in 1936 (Fig. 4 red next page). The resulting landslide dammed the river, backing the Middle Fork up to Big Snag Camp. Over a period of many years the lake filled with small gravels that were light enough to be carried through Dolly Lake at higher water. Several large trees along the river bank were drowned by the rising water (clue #1).

The Initial slide pinched the river into a narrow channel along the right bank. The constricted current created a 'fire hose" effect, increasing the speed and therefore erosive power of the river. Deflected by the slide, the waters chewed into the right bank leaving an exposed cross section of glacial fill (clue # 3). Immediately downstream, however, the waters slowed and deposited the newly acquired sediment. This created a broad shallow island that was an ideal spot to catch logs and other debris from the event (clue # 5).

The river eventually eroded through the slide leaving a cross section of the original jagged boulders along the left bank (clue #4). It continues to cut a sinewy path through the lake fill gravels upstream (clue #2), and several towering dead trees line the right bank providing clues to this relatively recent geologic event.

G12 - Mile 21.7 – Lake Creek Blowout: Wildfires in 2000 burned the entire Lake Creek drainage leaving the hillsides susceptible to erosion from heavy rains. A thunderstorm in August of 2001 triggered a debris flow that poured all the way across the Middle Fork. A second slide came down in 2003 covering the first . The river is slowly carving through the deposit and eroding into the left bank. (see Figs. 2 and 3 for a an erosion comparison) A fun class II+ wave train and tricky downstream gravel bar challenge boaters.

| *Figure 2 - 2002 Lake Creek slide after a peak water level of 5.81.* | *Figure 3 - 2003 Lake Creek slide after a peak water level of 8.18.* |

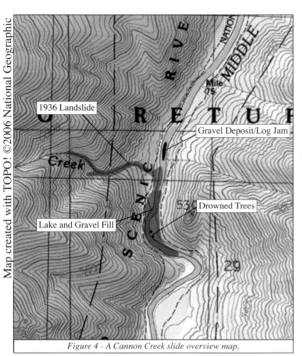

Figure 4 - A Cannon Creek slide overview map.

Labels on map:
- 1936 Landslide
- Gravel Deposit/Log Jam
- Drowned Trees
- Lake and Gravel Fill

G13 – Mile 22.1 – Constriction Rapid: Pistol Creek Rapid flows through a narrow constriction between vertical bedrock walls. Confining a river into a narrow channel increases its velocity. This effect is amplified at higher flows resulting in extremely powerful hydraulics. Constriction rapids like Pistol Creek, Ski Jump, and Cub Creek downstream tend to be some of the largest rapids at extreme flows.

G14 - Mile 22.8 – Fill Terraces: When Pistol Creek Ranch cabins first come into view look back upstream along the right bank. The 2000 fires cleared the trees to reveal a nice sequence of fill terraces.

G15 - Mile 26 – Landslide Remnant: The drainage on the right bank spewed a large debris fan into the river after the 2000 fires. There will be some remnant angular debris along the right bank and mixed into the bed load downstream from here.

G-16 Mile 26.6 – Fill Terraces: There are several significant terrace surfaces on the left bank at the downstream end of the Indian Creek airstrip. The highest is 320 feet above the river.

G17 - Mile 27 – Strath Terraces: Just above the mouth of Indian Creek on river right are some bedrock "strath" terraces. These flat surfaces cut into solid bedrock and are formed during periods of lateral erosion (see geology section for explanation). At low water a nice outcrop of some twisted, and folded rock can be seen at river level. This metamorphic rock will continue downstream through Pungo Canyon.

G18 - Mile 27.9 – Oreo Related Landslides: There are several small landslides that poured into the river on the inside right bank during thunderstorms in 2002. Can you pick out the remnant deposits being slowly disguised by the vegetation?

G19 - Mile 29.1 - Orelano Rapid and Landslide: Orelano Creek drains a steep, 3000 foot hillside in a landscape composed of broken, metamorphic rock. The drainage was badly burned in the 1979 Mortar Creek Fire. I have observed several small landslides come out of this creek over the years, but the most significant was in July of 2002. The narrow confines of Pungo Canyon focus the erosive power of the river. It removed much of the landslide after just one high water event. (See Figs. 5 and 6 for a before and after comparison.)

G 20 - Mile 31.2 – Mass Wasting: The term used to describe the annual erosion of material that falls into the river bed is "Mass Wasting". High water washes away sediment along the edge of the river. This undermines the steep hillsides above and both alluvial gravels and their vegetative cover fall into the river. There are several of these exposures along the river at the end of Pungo Canyon. The convenient removal of vegetation allows geologists a glimpse of the deposits underneath.

G 21 - Mile 31.7 – Fill Terraces: There are several well preserved glacial fill terraces at the end of Pungo Canyon. Three distinct levels are

Figure 5 - A view of the orelano slide in August of 2002.

Figure 6 - The same view in '03 after high water of 8.18 feet.

preserved on the inside bend across from Little Soldier Creek that sit 25, 50, and 100 feet above the river.

Figure 7 - The Thomas Creek glacial fill terraces.

G22 - Mile 32.5 – Bedrock Rapid: Marble Creek is a good example of a rapid formed by bedrock ledges in the river. Ledge hydraulics often form powerful re-circulating holes. The monster on the bottom right of Marble Creek (between 2.5 and 4.5 feet) is no exception.

G23 - Mile 35 – Thomas Creek Terraces: The opening of the landscape at Thomas Creek is caused by a change in the underlying geology. The resistant metamorphic rock encountered in Pungo Canyon gives way to the Casto Pluton Granites which will dominate the geology to the Flying B Ranch (with a notable exception in the Tappan Falls area).   The distinctive pink granite is composed of three minerals, Quartz, Potassium Feldspar (this gives the pink color), and Biotite. The Biotite flakes away easily, weakening the bonds between individual crystals causing exposed outcrops to break down rather quickly.

The erodable nature of this granite results in an open canyon landscape with few cliff walls. The hillsides are covered in a decomposed granitic soil which is easily saturated and prone to landslides during heavy rains.

Because the river is not confined between steep, narrow walls, the area around Thomas Creek contains an impressive display of glacial fill terraces. There are terraces on both sides of the river at 25, 55, 165, 280, and 370 feet above the river. (see Fig. 7). These large grass covered terraces prompted a succession of livestock operations to graze cattle and sheep along the river in the 1920's and 30's.

G24 – Mile 35.2 – Scarface Mountain: The steep, fire scarred slopes of Scarface Mountain has a small but noticeable landslide on its upper slopes. This scar is an erosion event related to the 1979 Mortar Creek Fire.

G25 - Mile 36.7 – Sunflower Fan Progression: The network of gullies feeding Sunflower Creek have been building a broad alluvial fan into the river for thousands of years. The small island and broad gravel shallows below Little Creek are probably remnants of gravel backfilling behind a small landslide dam. At some point, the river was deflected into the right bank, opposite the island and gnawed into the side of a glacial fill terrace.

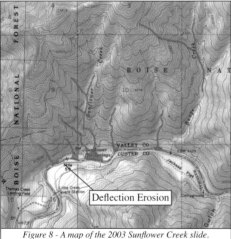

Figure 8 - A map of the 2003 Sunflower Creek slide.

A real life example of this progression occurred during a thunderstorm in 2002. Nearly every drainage in Sunflower Creek sent a river of debris downhill to converge on the broad alluvial fan (Fig. 8). Several huge boulders were deposited on the sloping surface above the water, and tongues of smaller debris extended into the river. Within two years, much of this material was covered with new vegetation and incorporated into the Sunflower fan.

G26 - Mile 37.7 – High Remnant Terrace: There is a possible remnant fill terrace nearly 1000 feet above the river on the left bank.

G27 - Mile 39.7 – Basalt Dikes: Black basalt dikes riddle much of the Middle Fork's bedrock geology. Several pink cliffs on the right bank between Lower Jackass Camp and Little Loon Creek display prominent dikes. These features will continue to crop up downstream.

G28 - Mile 41 – Fill Terraces: The flat bench that holds the Mahoney Airstrip on the left bank sits 320 feet above the river and is over 500,000 years old. The terrace itself is nearly covered in overburden from the hillsides above and is creased by several erosion gullies.

G29 - Mile 42.8 - Fred Paulson's Terrace: Like the American Indians before him, Fred Paulson probably built his cabin on this site because of the large terrace and available grassy feed for his pack animals.

G30 - Mile 44.9 – Red Bluff Rocks: There is an interesting juxtaposition here between the towering pink Casto Pluton cliff and several jet black boulders that dot the river. The boulders may have originated from a Basalt Dike somewhere in the vicinity.

G31 - Mile 48.1 – White Creek Terraces: The river is flanked on both sides by the 50 foot terrace associated with the last glacial filling event that ended 15 to 20,000 years ago. Figure 9 displays a nice terrace at the mouth of White Creek.

G 32 - Mile 49.2 – Gravel Islands: Several large gravel islands occupy the left turn below Shelf Camp. The 2002 Jack Creek landslide created a small lake that starts just below the islands. In three years I have watched this lake fill with a surprising amount of river gravel which has made me speculate on the origins of the islands upstream. Were they also deposited behind an historical landslide that has since eroded away, or does the wide stretch of river create a slower current that causes the river to drop it's bed load here?

G33 - Mile 49.7 – Imbrication: The Jack Creek debris fan has caused some impressive deflection erosion into the glacial terrace on the right bank. The exposed cross section displays the typical upstream sloping orientation of river deposited gravels. This phenomenon is called "Imbrication."

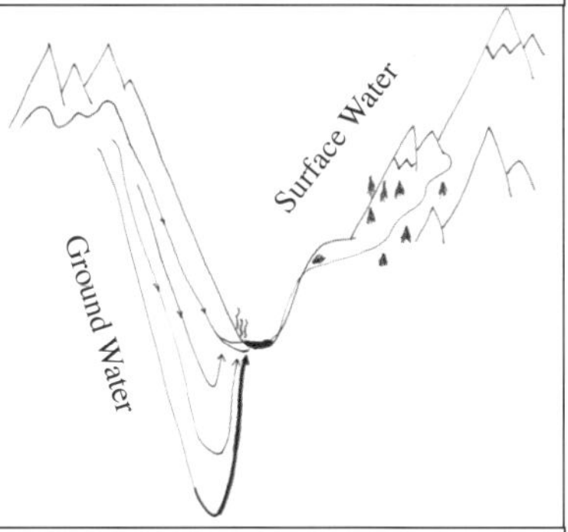

G34 - Mile 50.1 Thermal Hot Springs: Loon Creek Hot Springs is one of several that bubble up in the bottom of the Middle Fork canyon. The source for this hot water is not a geo-thermal "hot spot" underneath Idaho, but rather is caused by some well-insulated ground water.

Figure 9 - The White Creek terrace.

Figure 10 - A ground water cross section.

Water flowing underground mirrors the surface landscape. This means that steep mountains have a corresponding steep water table beneath the surface (Fig. 10). The hydrostatic pressure from a 3000 foot "mountain" of water will drive very deep circulation. Temperature increases 3 degrees Centigrade for every 100 meters of depth so it doesn't take much to heat water to a desirable temperature. If the hot water follows an independent route to the surface without losing it's heat by mixing with shallow flows, it emerges as a hot spring.

G35 - Mile 51.1 – Underwater Canyon: The river flows over a series of bedrock ledges about one mile below cow camp. At low water, rafts have to float over the underwater canyon to avoid hanging up on the shallow bedrock.

G36 - Mile 53.3 - Marble Outcrop: There are two white outcrops of rock that flank both sides of the river high above Horsetail Creek. These are deposits of metamorphosed limestone, better known as marble. These white rocks represent the first outcrop of the ancient "Belt Sediments" that once covered Idaho.

G37 - Mile 56.7 – Matamorphic Rocks: As the Grouse Necks drain into the pool above Grouse Creek Rapid there is a small cliff of swirled and twisted rock just above the water on river right. This is a dramatic exposure of metamorphic rock. This greenish, convoluted rock is both volcanic and sedimentary in origin and forms the bedrock in many of the Tappan Canyon rapids downstream.

G38 - Mile 57.1 - Grouse Creek Evoluion: Long term erosion of the broken metamorphic rocks in the Grouse Creek drainage has built a significant alluvial fan into the river channel. This has forced a migration of the channel to the north-west into the Casto Pluton granites as the river has cut deeper into the canyon (Fig. 11). This long term undercutting of the pink granite may explain this rare exposure of

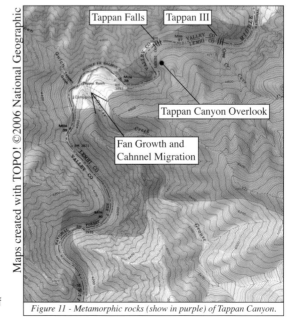
Maps created with TOPO! ©2006 National Geographic

Figure 11 - Metamorphic rocks (show in purple) of Tappan Canyon.

vertical Casto Pluton outcrops.

G39 - Mile 57.9 – Strath Terraces: Below 4 feet there are several metamorphic strath terraces exposed on both banks. The river is carving a new channel through this beautiful pink and green metamorphic rock.

G40 – Mile 58 - Tappan canyon overview: This explanation is best read after hiking to the Tappan Canyon Overlook (see hiking description for TF1 on page 72) which affords a wonderful perspective of the landscape.

Tappan Canyon is flanked on both sides by cliff walls that are dramatic for their vertical nature as well as the strikingly different color. This section of river is dominated by the beautiful green-gray Tappan Canyon Group (TCG) metamorphic rock that butts against the pink Casto Pluton granites. (Fig. 11 previous page) The more resistant TPG appears to have driven the incision of the Middle Fork westward along the contact zone between the two rocks. (see the geology map in Fig. 21 on page 93 for a broader perspective) The river follows the north-western edge of the TPG/Casto Pluton boundary before managing to cut into the resistant metamorphic rocks below Tappan Island.

The river then snakes back along the contact zone just above Tappan Falls before slicing an impressive vertical canyon through the Fish and Game Rock/Tappan III Rapid series. It is easy to pick out the contact between the two layers as the river turn towards Tappan Falls. All of the rapids in the canyon are created by TPG bedrock ledges or boulders that choke the river. The river emerges from Tappan Canyon and leaves the TCG rocks in the pool below Tappan IV Rapid.

G41 - Mile 62.8 – Casto Pluton Boulders: The vertical pink cliff along the left bank is the source for the large Casto Pluton boulders that dot the river below Funston Camp. Over time, several boulders of varying size have tumbled onto sloping bench along the bank and into the river. Can you identify the most recent addition (look for the jagged edges).

G42 - Mile 66.5 – Flying B Geology: The open canyon around the Flying B Ranch is again defined by underlying geology. The river cuts through a pocket of foliated granodiorite within a larger region of the Casto Pluton Granites. (see Fig. 21 on page 93) Contact zones between different rocks are more susceptible to erosion, especially in weaker granites like these. The severe erosion gives a more open feel to the canyon.

Large glacial fill terraces are preserved along the river. Several 270 foot surfaces are partially buried by the eroding hillside above and are cleaved by small gullies. The lowest benches provide the flat ground necessary for two backcountry airports.

G43 - Mile 67.8 – Haystack Evolution: The extensive debris fan at the mouth of Pole Creek has been building into the Middle Fork for thousands of years. This long-term alluvial fan deposition has pushed the river west, eroding into the base of the cliffs across the river (Fig. 12). The undermined wall is a likely source for the enormous boulders that litter the river channel today.

The Pole Creek debris flow happened the same season I was finishing my geology thesis so I have followed its evolution closely and have documented the changes with photographs. Prior to the Bernard Creek landslide in 2003, the "New Haystack" rapid was a challenging low water rapid. It also provided an opportunity to observe the river eroding through the landslide in real time. Figs. 13 - 15 and 16 - 17 provide a before and after photographic perspective.

Map created with TOPO! ©2006 National Geographic

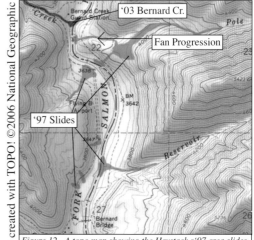

Figure 12 - A topo map showing the Haystack s'97 area slides.

Figure 13 - Haystack in Oct. '97, 2 months after the slide.

Figure 14 - Haystack in Aug. '01, 4 years later.

Figure 15 - Haystack in Aug. '03 after the Bernard slide.

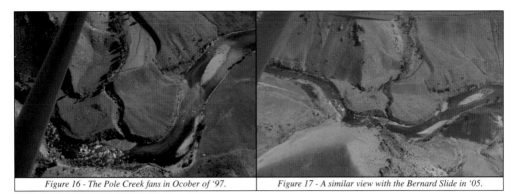

| Figure 16 - The Pole Creek fans in Ocober of '97. | Figure 17 - A similar view with the Bernard Slide in '05. |

G44 – Mile 67.9 - Bernard Creek Evolution: This fire related debris flow added another wrinkle to a geologically complex bend of the river. Will Haystack Rapid be forever flooded in the still waters behind the Bernard Creek fan? How long will it take the Middle Fork to clear this channel of sediment? How many times have these tributaries spilled debris into the river? These are among the many questions that will only be answered with the passage of time.

G45 - Mile 68.7 – Lower Canyon Entrance: Below Short Creek the character of the canyon changes abruptly. The river enters the "Yellowjacket Formation," an outcrop of the original "Belt Sediments" that were caught up in the tectonic collision 100 million years ago. These rocks are more compact than the granites around the Flying B Ranch. As a result, the walls in Jack Creek Canyon steepen dramatically.

G46 - Mile 72.5 – Land-slide Dam Sediments: The open and eroded topography between the Grassy I and II camps is caused by the erosion of sandy lake deposits laid down after the Cutthroat Cove landslide dammed the river (more detail is provided in the main geology section). Figure 18 shows a cross section of the two significant damming events at Cutthroat Cove and Weber Rapids. The lake was nearly 100 feet deep at Grassy I camp.

As the river dumped its sediment load into the still waters of the lake, only fine grained silts and marls made it the 5

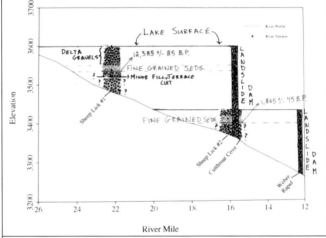

Figure 18 - A cross section showing the relationship between marl sediments and dams.

to 6 miles down to Grassy I. As the river delta at the head of the lake progressed downstream fine sands were carried to the camp, covering the marl deposits. These were topped by progressively heavier-grained sand and gravel. Finally, the whole column was capped with a layer of larger river rock.

In some places, this protective cap of gravels has protected the sand and marl deposits underneath, while in others it has not. If you dig into the hillsides behind Grassy I and II camps you will find a deep deposit of light gravels and sand. This soft material is being quickly eroded into the gentle hills found behind camp.

G47 – Marl Deposits: The pale soil beneath the large ponderosa tree contains the most concentrated deposit of a calcium carbonate marl. These layers were laid down after the Cutthroat Cove slide dammed the river. In some exposures you can identify additional layers that correspond to seasonal spring runoff.

G48 - Mile 74 – Rattlesnake Cave Contact: There is a distinct contact between an igneous intrusion of pink porphoritic granite and dark sedimentary rock on the wall of the cave. The pictographs are drawn on the pink granite. Notice the large, rectangular feldspar crystals which developed during a period of slow cooling. These are surrounded by a matrix of very small, grayish crystals that solidified almost instantly when the magma was intruded into the surrounding rock.

Look along the river right cliff wall when leaving the cave to see the compact horizontal layers preserved from the original sedimentation. Across the river are folded sedimentary layers that have been tilted on end to form a pointy rock spire.

G49 - Mile 74.5 – Ripple Marks: Evidence of the depositional environment are preserved in the cliff wall below Wollard Camp. At low water, row along the river left cliff wall to get a close up view of ripple marks that were created by water flowing over the pre-historic "Belt Sediments."

91

G50 - Mile 75.3 – Ripple Marks: There is another exposure of ripple marks on the left wall below Kimmel Creek Rapid.

G51 - Mile 76 – Idaho Batholith Granite: Just below "Sams Hole" rapid the river leaves the sedimentary "Belt Sediments" behind and enters a long stretch of the Idaho Batholith Granites. Note the uniform salt and pepper look of this formation that will dominate the corridor for nearly 10 miles. This rock likely originated from the Pacific Ocean plate that melted beneath Idaho 100 million years ago (see geology map in Fig. 21 next page)

G52 - Mile 77.4 – Imbrication: The large gravel bar that runs from Fish Camp to just above Waterfall Creek Rapid offers a good example of "Imbrication." The river organizes its bed load of gravels into a position of least resistance. If you look across the gravel bar from the side you can see a diagonal trend to the deposit. The rocks present a smooth face to the oncoming current which makes them less likely to get tumbled downstream. Walk onto the gravel bar at low water and see if you can notice a difference when looking upstream versus downstream.

G53 - Mile 78.7 - Cutthroat Cove Landslide Dam: When approaching Cutthroat Cove Rapid from the pool upstream, look for the flat dam surface about 200 feet above the right side of the river. The landslide poured into the river from a gully on the left bank between upper and lower Cutthroat Cove Rapid. As you approach Big Pine Camp around the corner look back upstream to see the cliff escarpment left behind from the rock slide (see Fig. 18 on page 91 for a cross section diagram of the dam).

G54 - Mile 79.3 and 79.5 - Elk Bar Sheep Licks: This second calcium carbonate marl is preserved in a rocky terrace across and downstream from Love Bar Camp. This deposit was laid down 1800 years ago from a landslide at Weber Rapid. It is easy to miss if you are not paying attention

G55 – Mile 79.5 – Basalt Dikes: There are several horizontal bands of dark basalt dikes that cut through the impressive cliff wall above Love Bar Camp. These are similar to dikes that were noted below the Jackass Camps.

G56 - Mile 80.6 – Wall Creek Debris Fan: Though it is sometimes difficult to focus on geology when approaching a major rapid, notice the large accumulation of boulders and other debris coming out of Wall Creek. The long term accumulation of material at the mouth of side canyons creates many of the rapids on the Middle Fork.

G57 - Mile 82.6 – Weber Landslide Dam: The second of two significant landslide dams occurred at this rapid 1,800 years ago. A chunk of the cliff wall collapsed from river right (Fig. 19 red). The resulting lake filled with sediment burying a second calcium carbonate marl upstream near Love Bar Camp. In this narrow stretch of canyon, the river managed to remove the entire deposit leaving only the remnants that create Weber Rapid.

G58 - Mile 83 – Metamorphic Gneiss: As the canyon turns left below Mist Falls notice another change in the geology and character of the canyon (see the geology map in Fig. 21) Gone are the vertical salt and pepper walls of the white Idaho Batholith Granite. The river enters a zone of metamorphic "Gneiss." As the molten Idaho Batholith rose beneath Idaho 100 million years ago it created a zone of intense "contact metamorphism" of twisted, folded, and banded rock. The river crosses this boundary below Mist Falls. The canyon walls, though still dramatically steep, are composed of tortured metamorphic rock from here to the Main Salmon.

G59 - Mile 84.1 – Ship Island Wall: The vertical cliff face behind Ship Island camp is a beautiful example of metamorphic rock. Layers of dark and light (and even some green) gneissic banding is evident on a large scale. You can even pick out some white granitic intrusions that likely originated from the molten Idaho Batholith. There is a large water worn metamorphic boulder upstream of camp that is worth a look and a quite moment of contemplation.

G60 - Mile 84.3 – Lower Canyon Terrace: One of the few fill terraces that is preserved in the steep walled Impassable Canyon can be seen below the mouth of Ship Island Creek on river right. It is mostly covered by "overburden" or rocky material falling from the hillside above, but a distinct flat plane can be seen about 40 feet above the rivers edge.

G61 – Mile 85.2 – Boudinage: French for "sausage" this term describes a geologic feature that is formed from intense pressure stretching of metamorphic rocks. As a particular layer of vein tries to stay together, it will stretch thin in places forming a series of sausage links. There is a good example of this on the left bank just below the Ship Island turn.

G62 - Mile 85.1 - Turn Below Ship Island: The 90 degree right turn below Ship Island Camp affords one of the most beautiful views on the river. The sloping ramps downstream right are likely the result of large scale faulting in the region. Ramps with similar orientation are found throughout Impassable Canyon. Look downstream to see the top of the Parrot Placer landslide.

G63 - Mile 86 - Parrot Placer Slide: The Ship Island fire in 1979 burned the hillside above the camp. Rain falling on the steep mountain slopes have produced numerous small landslides over the years, once spilling a slurry of sand and gravel into the tents of a group camped for the night.

Watch out here during a heavy rainstorm.

G64 - Mile 88.5 – "Gneissly Water Polished":
Not very often do we get to see the "true colors" of the rocks in the Middle Fork canyon. The surface is usually covered with vegetation, a weathered patina, or a wide variety of lichen species. The inside wall of Lower Cliffside rapid is a rare exception. Washed clean at high water, this beautiful exposure of metamorphic banded Gneiss is well worth a quick glimpse over your left shoulder mid-rapid.

G65 - Mile 89.6 Vertical Layering: As you approach the turn at Cliffside camp, take note of the vertical layering of plates on the left bank. This is probably the original sedimentary layering that has been preserved through the metamorphic process.

G66 - Mile 89.9 – Preserved Terrace: 1000 feet above the water on river left is a rare, flat bench. It may be a remnant river terrace associated with a historical Stoddard Creek alluvial fan. I finally hiked to the flat in 2005 but could not locate any river cobbles on the bench surface. A 1000 foot fill terrace would likely date back 2 million years to early Middle Fork history.

G67 - Mile 91.9 – Old Landslide Rapid: Hancock rapid is the longest on the river. This is due to the close proximity of Nolan Creek (river left) with Roaring Creek (river right). Both tributaries have built opposing debris piles into the river to create a long, and challenging boulder garden.

G68 - Mile 92.1 – Sculpted Rock: Below Hancock Rapid on the right bank (low water) is some beautifully eroded rock. At extremly high water, the power of the micro eddies actually form pressure cavities that pluck away at solid rock. This "cavitation erosion" creates some very pretty sculptures.

G69 - Mile 92.5 – Sedimentary Plates: Though officially metamorphic rocks, you can see what may be the original sedimentary layering in the rocks on the left bank. These impressive plates are standing on end and form an impressive spire below Solitude Camp.

G70 – Best Rock On The Middle Fork: The BROT-MF is visible at moderate to low water. The impressive squiggly vein on the top right side of the boulder is a result of the intense metamorphic pressure placed on these rocks. Just like a folded deck of playing cards, rocks on the inside of geologic bends are put under intense pressure. The is simply not enough space to deform evenly so some rocks contort into intense squiggles to relieve the pressure.

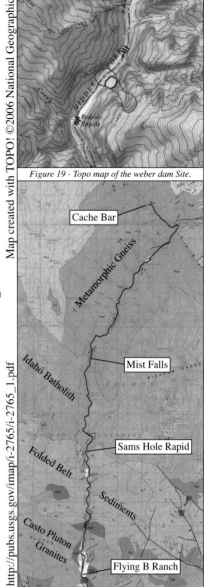

Figure 19 - Topo map of the weber dam Site.

Map created with TOPO! ©2006 National Geographic

Geology map courtesy of http://pubs.usgs.gov/imap/i-2765/i-2765_1.pdf

Figure 21 - The Lower Canyon geologic map.

G71 - Mile 94.7 – Granite Intrusion: A granite intrusion forms blocky cliffs along the right side of Goat Creek Rapid. Try to pick out the vein as it continues across to the other side of the river.

Below this vein to the confluence the rocks have a reflective quality and appear more brittle in nature than the folded gneiss. You are floating away from the heat source of the Idaho batholith and into reflective schist rocks.

G72 - Mile 98 – Cramer Creek Blowout: This is the most recent and notorious addition to the canon of Middle Fork Rapids. "The Dreaded" Cramer Creek used to be a fun, deep, Class II+ wave train we would swim on a hot afternoon. In 2003 an intense fire burned the headwaters of Cramer Creek (two fire fighters from Salmon were killed in the suppression efforts). Later that year a thunderstorm triggered a landslide that dumped significant debris into the river. The initial rapid was best run along the left bank, but high water has washed a channel out along the right side. Watch out for the giant hole in the center.

Notes